How to Make
Cloth Dolls

How to Make
Cloth Dolls

Jan Horrox

SEARCH PRESS

First published in 2020

Search Press Limited
Wellwood, North Farm Road,
Tunbridge Wells, Kent TN2 3DR

How to Make Cloth Dolls uses material from the following
books by Jan Horrox published by Search Press:
Introduction to Making Cloth Dolls, 2010
Making Fantasy Cloth Dolls, 2013

Suppliers
For details of suppliers, please visit the Search Press
website: www.searchpress.com
Alternatively, materials can be supplied worldwide
via the author's own website: www.janhorrox.co.uk

Publishers' notes
All the step-by-step photographs in this book feature
the author, Jan Horrox, demonstrating how to make
cloth dolls. No models have been used.

**These dolls are not designed as play dolls and,
because of the small parts involved, are not
suitable for children under five years old.**

Acknowledgements
I would like to thank Katie French, my
editor, for all her work and enthusiasm;
Roddy Paine Photographic Studio for their
wonderful photography; Ray Slater for
her introduction to cloth dolls; Justine
Williamson for her constant help and support
throughout; and Sarah Slade for
her exceptional technical skills in helping
with the preparation of the projects.

Contents

Miranda 40

Peaseblossom 54

Anastasia 68

Morwenna 86

Titania 100

Nerissa 114

Introduction

Dolls have been objects of interest and creativity well back into ancient history. The modern-day cloth doll incorporates many technical skills and levels of design associated with the textile arts that are so popular today. For those wishing to expand their craft skills into cloth-doll making, or for those who wish to make a fairly simple cloth doll, you will find all you need in this book.

Fantasy plays such an important part in modern life, and thus several of the projects in this book are inspired by this genre. Much of our media – books, films, games, television and role play – is centred upon the fantasy themes that many of us find so fascinating. Cloth dolls are perfect for allowing us to explore our imaginations and create fabulous, dreamlike figures from fabric and stitch.

My personal journey began with a training in fashion/textiles, after which I spent a career in fashion design. I became captivated with cloth-doll making several years ago when looking for a new outlet for my particular experience and skills. Cloth dolls offer everyone an exciting opportunity to combine many varied craft techniques in one project, which will at the same time develop a fascinating personality of its own.

All the basic techniques for cloth-doll making are described in simple steps, with useful sections on creating hair, stuffing techniques, and making hands, heads and faces. Some simple methods for fabric colouring are also included, with an emphasis on using recycled or everyday household items. Further instructions on embroidery and embellishment are included with each project. As you work your way through the book, do not be afraid to experiment with colour and texture; try out different fabrics, embellishments and paint effects; and, using the templates provided, create beautiful fantasy dolls of your own.

The book contains six different projects for 40–46cm (16–18in) dolls, each with a second doll that is made using the same methods as the first but in a different colour scheme. The parts of all the dolls are interchangeable. The designs therefore lend themselves to interpretation, allowing you to use your creative skills to develop unique dolls of your own.

Materials & equipment

To create the cloth dolls in this book you will benefit from having the specified woven fabrics as well as certain equipment and tools. There are a few tools and haberdashery items that are well worth having, but many items can be improvised to begin with.

I always work with high-count woven cotton fabric for the bodies, heads, arms, legs, hands and feet – in other words, all the 'flesh' parts. I find this type of cotton fabric, which is known as Pimatex cotton, sculpts well and provides a good surface for drawing on. Sometimes the body parts are made directly from decorative fabrics and not costumed separately.

You will probably have a stash of fabrics and fibres that you can draw from for costuming, hair and trimmings. To create an exciting collection of dolls you will want to build up a diverse selection of small quantities of prints, silks, lace, novelty fabrics, ribbons and trims. Look out for interesting pieces at fairs and in charity shops or thrift stores to supplement your collection. Patchwork and quilting shops will stock a good range of prints and silks in fat quarters. All kinds of fibres and furs can be used for hair – the more unusual types are the most striking. Look out for interesting trims, buttons, shells, beads, charms and small dried flowers.

Everything can be found on the internet from specialist doll-making, art and fabric suppliers. In times when independent retailers are disappearing fast, the internet provides an excellent means of sourcing materials and tools. If you don't like ordering online, many online suppliers will allow you to order over the phone. Pens and pencils for face colouring can be bought from good art suppliers. Textile dyes and paints for colouring fabrics can be obtained from specialist textile craft suppliers.

Materials for making the bodies and heads

I use a fine-woven, high-count Pimatex cotton for all the 'flesh' parts, and stuff them with a good-quality polyester filling. Pimatex cotton moulds well and provides an excellent surface for drawing and colouring the dolls' faces. It is the best woven fabric to use for five-fingered hands, being the strongest and softest to use for fingers. A good-quality patchwork or quilting cotton can work well too, and is available in a large range of skin colours. Pimatex is now available only in white so I dye all my fabric to a pale skin shade. The recipe for dyeing Pimatex fabric a pale flesh tone using Dylon® washing-machine dye is given right.

Don't be tempted to use a poor-quality fabric such as calico or a coarse, loosely woven cotton just because it looks attractive. You will find it wrinkles or doesn't stand the strain of the stuffing and the seams will burst. This is very frustrating when you have spent considerable time making a head or hand. Cloth dolls are stuffed very firmly so always use a strong fabric for any body part.

There are a number of other knitted fabrics used for cloth-doll making that you might like to experiment with. Craft velour is a polyester-knit fabric with a pile on one side and a one-way stretch. It is very popular and is excellent for sculpted character dolls such as trolls or elves. Doe or buck suede is a similar fabric that is a little heavier and not available in such a varied colour range. Cotton jersey is a tubular, fairly firm knitted fabric, made of 100 per cent cotton, which is available in skin shades. It sculpts well but is difficult to draw on, so you will need to vary the techniques you use for adding the facial features. Cotton lycra is similar to cotton jersey in its use.

Assorted types of face and body fabrics in various flesh tones. A couple of knitted fabrics are included with a selection of fine-woven cotton fabrics. The three main threads I use for constructing the dolls are extra-strong upholstery thread for jointing, quilting thread for needle-sculpting and polyester thread for machining. Use good quality supersoft polyester stuffing for filling the dolls.

Decorative fabrics & trimmings

Fabric colouring, painting and embroidery are applied to the fabrics before the doll parts are cut out and stitched together. The costume and clothing for cloth dolls are not usually made separately – they are all part of the body construction. Skirts, ruffles, wings, beading, jewellery, ribbons and hair are all added to the doll when partly or totally assembled. This is the fun part of the process after you have put in the hard work of making the doll's head, face and body parts.

Cotton batiks are excellent for cloth-dolls' bodies and are readily available from specialist patchwork and quilting shops or online retailers. They come in a broad range of wonderful colours and designs, and form an inspiring base fabric to embellish with stitch, paint or beading. Make sure you use a good-quality batik that is strong enough to hold the stuffing. Polyester organzas are low-cost alternatives and come in gorgeous, vibrant colours as well as soft shades. These are very useful for doll costuming and wings.

Accessories like scarves, lace or fish-net tights and patterned socks are available from markets and budget stores and are very affordable. These are excellent for all types of garments and doll accessories, including stockings, mittens, sweaters and headgear.

Your fabric collection should also include a good selection of felt pieces in a range of colours, pieces of soft leather and novelty fabrics such as metallics or lace. All these can be sourced from markets, second-hand stores and craft sales. Try entering what you need into your internet browser – you will almost always find exactly what you want.

Polyester tulles come in many vibrant colours. Small pieces of polyester lace and cotton lace can be dyed and painted, and polyester ribbons in 7mm (¼in) or 3mm (⅛in) widths, available in a huge range of colours, make pretty additions to any costume. White ribbons can be painted with textile paint and then tiny buttons or beads sewn on them for decoration. Look out for novelty trims at sales and in charity/op shops or thrift stores. Often you can take something apart and re-use the pieces. Assorted beads, sequins and buttons will all add sparkle. Angelina hot-fix fibres fuse together to produce a sheet of sparkling gossamer that is especially good for wings. It can be combined with sheer nylon organzas or tulles, and jewellery wire added for support.

Tip

Fabrics are often bought in fat quarters. These are pre-cut squares usually measuring around 46 x 46cm (18 x 18in) – a useful quantity for cloth-doll making.

Cotton prints, cotton batiks and dupion silks are available in a wonderful range of colours and designs.

A mass of brightly coloured polyester organzas and tulles for costuming. Look out for sequinned dance fabrics.

Embellishments

Embellishments are great fun – they are the all-important finishing touches that will make a real difference to the look and style of your doll. Collect fancy printed ribbons and trims for your stash. These can be used to accent your doll's costuming and can bring the doll to life. Satin ribbons in 7mm (¼in) or 3mm (⅛in) widths are available in a huge range of colours.

Angelina fibres are delicate, iridescent fibres that are perfect for adding a touch of sparkle to your fantasy doll. Mix standard Angelina with other fibres to enliven your doll's hair, or use the hot-fix variety to create beautiful, shimmering fabric for fairy wings (see page 13).

Some shells have tiny natural holes in them, but drilled shells are available online. Alternatively, try drilling your own or look for plastic shells instead. Dried flowers, ribbon flowers and silk and organza flowers are a pretty addition; you can make your own silk or organza flowers following the instructions on page 62. Charms in pewter or other metals can also be used to enhance your doll.

Other items for your ever-growing stash are buttons and beads in a size suitable for decorating cloth dolls. Look out for these in specialist shops, charity shops or thrift stores, craft fairs and on online auction sites, and remember that old items of clothing and jewellery are a rich source of interesting embellishments for cloth dolls.

Materials for hair

Cloth-doll hair can be as natural or as wild and fantastical as you like. For a more natural look, use synthetic hair or mohair fibres; for something more exotic, use any interesting fibre or yarn you can find. Synthetic hair can be great fun to use – it is easy to handle, easy to attach and cheap to buy. It comes in a range of colours and textures, from silky and straight to curly, and can be dressed in whatever style you like. Mohair fibre and braids are sold specifically for dolls' hair. These can be stitched or needle-felted on to the head. They come in a variety of natural colours and make very pretty, soft hair with a nice sheen.

There is a huge variety of fancy chunky yarns now available and these make excellent dolls' hair, for example sari silk, chunky slub yarn, eyelash yarn, ribbon yarn and chunky wool. All are simple to apply and reasonably priced, and you may well have a large assortment in your stash already. There is a particular type of yarn used by experienced cloth-doll makers, known as Yadeno mohair. It is a special, beautifully dyed mohair from Australian and Tibetan lamb skins, which comes in a variety of dyed colours, both natural and bright. It makes beautiful wigs, and is particularly suitable for fairy-type dolls. It is, however, fairly expensive and is only available from specialist suppliers. Fur fabric can also be used, but is not so effective and does not take dye or paint.

Colouring & altering fabrics

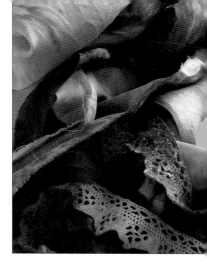

There are many ways of colouring and changing the nature of a fabric to make it even more magical. Dyeing and painting opens up a whole world of creativity and can be used to add colour to plain fabrics and give an individual look to your doll. There are many fabric paints and dyes readily available from specialist fabric art suppliers and also, quite often, from hardware shops. These usually come with instructions. Natural fibres, such as cotton and silk, are easiest to work with and give the best results. Experiment on some remnants of fabric before starting a whole project.

Layering and heating are other popular ways of altering fabrics. These techniques lend themselves particularly well to fairy wings – use them to give some stiffness as well as texture, and then add metallic edges or gilding flakes. Lumiere® is a beautiful range of metallic and pearlescent textile paints from Jacquard. It comes in a variety of colours, available in small amounts in bottles with spouts, making the colours easy to apply and draw with.

Painting ribbons and trims

Decorate ribbons and trims by painting on stripes or stamping with stars, circles or other shapes; pin out the ribbon to keep it steady. When dry, iron on the back of the ribbon with a hot iron to fix. You can then add beads, buttons or embroidery to complete your unique trims.

Block printing natural fabric pieces

This method will work well for any natural fabrics, such as cotton or silk. Here I have used Jacquard textile paint in violet and Jacquard Lumiere® in gold, and applied them to the block using a foam brush. Alternatively, you can roll out the paint on to a laminated sheet using a brayer (roller) and then dip the block into the paint. Begin by covering your table with plastic. Use wet wipes for cleaning your equipment and your hands afterwards.

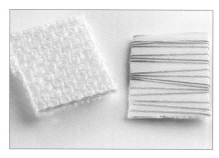

1 Make your block by wrapping bubblewrap around a piece of thick card or foam board, about 8 x 12cm (3¼ x 4¾in). Secure it in place and leave a 'handle' at the back. You may prefer to create a different type of block by wrapping medium-weight string around it.

2 Spoon some textile paint into a plastic container. Holding the block at the back, pick up some paint with the foam brush and paint it on to the block. Make sure the block is evenly coated with dye.

3 Place the inked block firmly on to the fabric. Repeat this as required to create your design. When the first coat is dry you can overprint with a second colour. When thoroughly dry, iron the back with a hot iron to fix the colour.

Altering organza

Polyester organza is a low-cost and versatile synthetic fabric much used in textile art because it responds to heat in very interesting ways. Applying heat using a craft heat gun will initially create a bubbly surface then, as more heat is applied, the fabric will begin to melt and small holes will appear. The whole process takes only a few seconds. It's important to hold the heat gun 20.5–25.5cm (8–10in) from the surface and keep it moving all the time to avoid burning (see the photographs right).

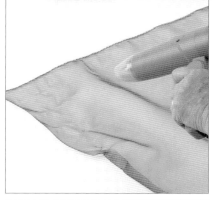

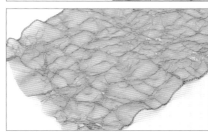

Using Angelina

Angelina is a synthetic fibre which comes in two types – standard and hot-fix. Standard Angelina can be mixed with other hair fibres and needle-felted into a doll's head as hair. The hot-fix variety makes a delicately shimmering fabric for fairy wings (see right) or the top layer of organza flowers. Try mixing two different colours together for a variegated effect.

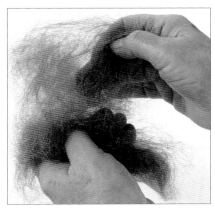

1 Begin by teasing the hot-fix Angelina into a very fine layer.

2 Lay the Angelina on your ironing board, sandwiched between two layers of baking parchment to protect your iron and the surface of your ironing board. Press with a hot iron for a few seconds.

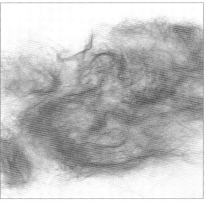

3 Remove the top layer of baking parchment to reveal the layer of heat-fused Angelina fibres underneath.

Tools and equipment

Most of the tools and equipment listed below are available from general art and craft suppliers and haberdashery shops. The more specialist items can be bought from doll-making and quilting suppliers, including internet and mail-order companies.

Sewing machine

Your sewing machine will need to have an open quilting/appliqué foot or a clear foot in order to sew around intricate pattern shapes like fingers. Always use a small stitch size (1–2, depending upon the type of machine). This enables you to stitch around small pieces and also makes a strong seam. You will need good, sharp machine needles suitable for cotton fabrics, size 80/12.

Scissors

You will need sharp-pointed embroidery scissors; good, sharp fabric scissors for cutting out fabric pieces; and a pair of paper scissors.

Needles

Doll needles, used for jointing the doll together, usually come in sets of two or three and are approximately 18cm (7in), 12cm (4¾in) and 7cm (2¾in) long. Long, fine darning needles in size 7 are also useful, and an assortment of long, fine darning needles in sizes 1 to 5 are ideal for sculpting the face. Felting needles, gauge 36 or 40, can be used for felting fibres into the cloth-doll head to make hair. You will also need a selection of ordinary sewing needles suitable for hand-stitching.

Glass-headed pins

These are used for marking the points on the needle-sculpted face before stitching, and for securing fabric, trims, ribbon, etc. before stitching.

Threads

You will need quilting thread for needle-sculpting the face and for ladder stitch (used for closing seams after stuffing); good-quality polyester threads for machine stitching fabrics; and an extra-strong upholstery thread capable of withstanding the strain of jointing the limbs and body together – it can be mortifying if it snaps halfway through the process!

Forceps or hemostats

Hemostats (medical forceps) are an excellent tool for the cloth-doll maker. They come in a wide range of sizes, but I find about 12cm (5in) the most useful. Use them for turning the doll pieces, for smoothing through the seams when turned and for pushing stuffing into the difficult-to-reach places. Forceps are available from cloth-doll suppliers and fishing shops.

Stuffing tool

This is specifically designed for pushing the stuffing into the various doll parts. A chopstick is a good substitute to begin with.

Finger-turning tools

These are sets of brass rods and tubes made specially for turning dolls' fingers. They fit together like a telescope so that you have a good choice of sizes to fit different-sized fingers.

Vanishing fine-line pen (air-drying)

This is used for drawing out the features of the face (see page 22) and for marking fingers on the mitt hand. Make sure the ink is air-drying and does not need washing out – putting water on your doll's face will ruin it.

Mechanical or sharp pencil (H or HB)

For tracing your templates on to the fabric, you need to draw a fine pencil line that will not show on the right side. A white watercolour pencil is useful for drawing on to dark fabrics.

Fabric eraser

A useful tool for removing unwanted pencil marks.

Seam sealant

Fray Check or Fray Stoppa are seam sealants used particularly for sealing finger seams before turning. It can be useful if you have a weak seam or have cut too close to the seam. Alternatively, PVA glue can be used instead.

Chenille sticks (pipe cleaners)

Available in packs in white or cream, sizes 6mm (¼in), 9mm (⅜in) and 12mm (½in), these are usually 30cm (12in) long and used for wiring the fingers.

Baking parchment

Purchased in a roll, baking parchment is used to protect your iron and your ironing board when ironing Angelina fibres. Used as a protective layer, it prevents the synthetic fibres from sticking to the iron or to the board. It is very useful in many textile processes.

Wired designer cord

This cotton-covered wire is used for edging fairy wings or in any project where you need to strengthen and sculpt an edge. It is available in various colours.

Soldering iron

Specially designed soldering irons are available for textile artists for use with synthetic fabrics. They are a good investment for anyone interested in modern textured techniques.

Craft glue

You will find a good, general craft glue such as Tacky Glue very useful, for example for making boots and wings and helping to attach hair and heads.

Heat gun

This item is much used for heating synthetic fabrics such as organza, tulle and Tyvek for decorative use. Always use a heat gun in a well-ventilated space and never heat polystyrene. Heat guns are available from many craft suppliers and are widely used in modern textile work.

Ruler

A small, clear plastic ruler with measurements in metric and imperial is very useful for marking seam allowances.

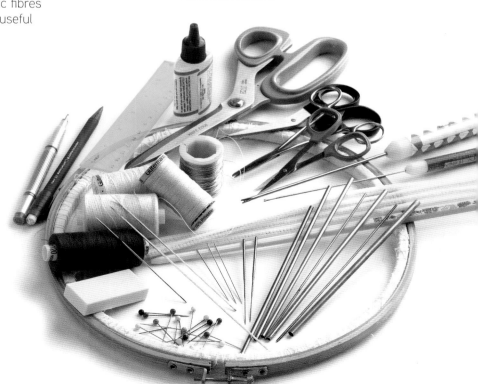

Face-colouring equipment

When starting to make cloth dolls, many people feel daunted by the face colouring. By following these instructions as carefully as possible you will be surprised how easy it is to achieve a good result. The more faces you paint the more confident you will become. Try to make three heads for each doll you make and then choose the best one. This way you will get plenty of practice and soon become very proficient in drawing faces. You can then progress on to developing your own style and colours.

It is advisable to use the equipment listed here to get the best results. Fine Pigma Micron pens will not run on fabric and the soft watercolour pencil crayons can be blended together to create a wonderfully artistic, coloured face using cotton buds/swabs or a piece of soft cloth.

White acrylic paint and fine paintbrushes are used for painting eye whites and highlights on to your dolls' faces.

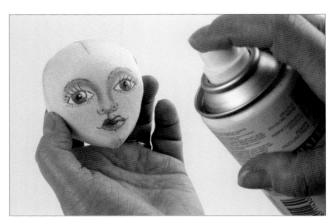

Artist's fixative spray is used for fixing faces after colouring them. Hold the can 25–32cm (10–12in) away from the face for spraying.

Fine-line Pigma Micron pens

These are available in various thicknesses and are used for drawing on your dolls' faces. I use a size 005 (0.2mm) for the first outline and size 01 (0.25mm) for filling in when I am sure of the lines I have drawn. You need both these sizes in black and brown for outlining the features, and perhaps red for mouths and blue or green for irises, though all these colours are not necessary to begin with. These pens are waterproof and will not run on fabric.

Watercolour pencil crayons

These are used for putting colour on to the dolls' faces, usually after the features are drawn in. They are softer than the pens and blend better on the fabric. I use them dry, not dampened. Prismacolour pencil crayons are very soft and blend beautifully, though they are not easily available. A good basic set to start with is burnt ochre, terracotta, goldenrod, grape, pink blush and cream for the skin colours; scarlet lake and crimson for the mouths; and a good light and dark blue or green for the irises. I also use dark umber, light umber, yellow ochre, carmine red, process red, magenta and white. As you gain more experience, you will develop your own preferred colour schemes.

Vanishing fine-line pen (air-drying)

This is used for drawing out the features of the face, so that if you are not happy with the result it will disappear and you can start again (see page 22). Make sure the ink is air-drying and does not need washing out – putting water on your doll's face will ruin it.

White Fabricolour pen

This pen delivers an opaque, white ink that is ideal for highlights and eye whites. It avoids having to use acrylic paint and a brush, which can be tricky.

Pigma brush pens

These are similar to the fine-line Pigma Micron pens. They can be used like a pen or like a brush to paint with. They are useful for drawing the eyes and eye sockets on to a face that has an acrylic-painted surface, for example Morwenna the steampunk doll on pages 86–97.

Scalpel

Watercolour pencils are very soft so I sharpen them carefully using a scalpel so as not to damage the colour centres. You will need to keep your pencils sharp for accenting.

Gesso and acrylic paint

To achieve a deathly white skin tone, I paint the body using white gesso for the undercoat and white acrylic paint for the second and third coats. White gesso is commonly used for coating a canvas before painting with acrylic paints.

Sandpaper

Fine-grade sandpaper is used for sanding the gesso and the acrylic paint when dry before applying the next coat.

Watercolour paints

A small set of basic watercolour paints is useful for adding a colour wash to an acrylic-painted head.

Brushes

I use a ½in (13mm) flat brush for the head and flesh parts, a size 4 pointed brush for the features and a size 8 round brush for applying a colour wash.

Basic techniques

In this section, I will describe the basic techniques that I use for transferring the templates to the fabric and for stitching and stuffing the body pieces.

All the pattern pieces are reproduced actual size on pages 128–143. You can trace them on to copy paper or photocopy them on to card. These should then be cut out carefully and accurately so that you can trace around them on to the fabric. Card patterns can be re-used and will last a long time. They are also a little firmer to draw around.

The pattern lines, i.e. the edges of the pattern pieces, are also the sewing lines, and the seam allowance is outside these lines. In most cases you will trace the pattern shapes on to doubled fabric with a mechanical or sharp HB pencil, stitch on the pattern lines and then cut out the shape. The seam allowance for a stitched seam is 3mm (1/8in) and for a seam to be sewn after cutting the allowance is 6mm (1/4in).

Reverse the stitching at the beginning and end of each seam to lock the ends of the seams, and use a clear or open foot on your sewing machine so that you can follow the pattern lines easily. A small stitch size of 1–2 is ideal for stitching the seams.

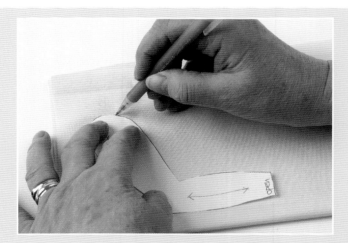

1 Lay the pattern piece on to a piece of doubled fabric, aligning it with the grain of the fabric if necessary. Draw around the pattern piece carefully and accurately with a propelling or sharp HB pencil. This is the line that you will sew along.

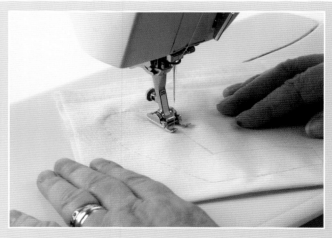

2 Remove the pattern piece and machine stitch around the drawn line, leaving any openings where marked for stuffing or inserting other body parts. Use the open or clear foot on your machine and a small stitch size – about 1–2, depending upon the type of machine. This enables you to stitch around small pieces and also makes a strong seam.

Stuffing

You will need a tool for stuffing – either a chopstick or a stuffing tool – and a pair of 12cm (5in) forceps or hemostats. Use good-quality polyester stuffing as this will not go lumpy. Start with a good handful of stuffing and push it into the centre of the piece.

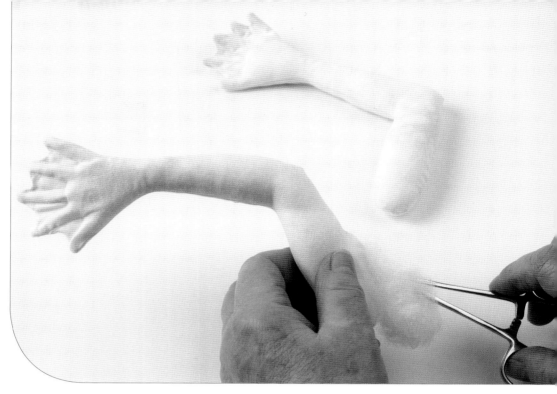

Small pieces of stuffing tend to clump, so if you use relatively large pieces your doll will be less lumpy. Push the piece of stuffing into the body part with your chosen tool. Fill the edges of the piece first then keep pushing stuffing into the centre and teasing it out to fill all the crevices. These dolls are stuffed very firmly and you will be surprised at the amount of stuffing used for a fairly small piece. You are aiming to achieve a smooth and firm finish.

After stuffing, use ladder stitch to close the opening. Thread a normal sewing needle with polyester thread, fasten the thread at the beginning of the opening and work the stitch as shown right. Pull the thread taut every few stitches and the opening will close up invisibly (see also pages 42–43).

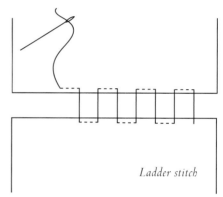

Ladder stitch

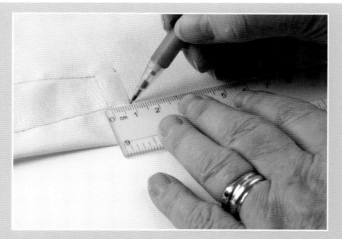

3 On the seams that are left open and will be stitched later, mark 6mm (¼in) seam allowances using a pencil and ruler. The remaining 3mm (⅛in) seams are judged by eye as you cut and do not require marking.

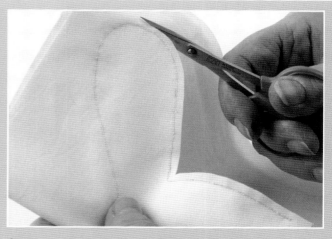

4 Cut around the shape using a pair of small, sharp-pointed scissors, leaving the appropriate seam allowances.

Making heads & faces

Miranda (pages 40–52) has a head made in three parts with a flat face. This head is simple to make but needs a little care when plotting out the face before drawing on the features. The other five dolls have needle-sculpted heads, which gives them a three-dimensional face; the needle-sculpting is done before drawing the features.

Flat faces

Making the head

This type of head is made with three pieces of fabric. The front is one piece cut on the fold and the back is two pieces cut on the bias.

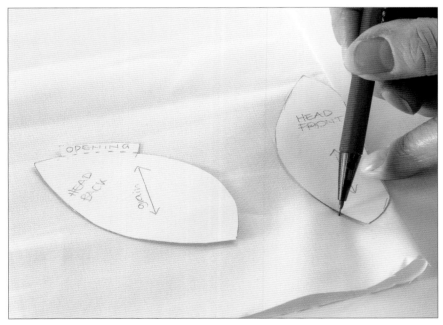

1 Place the two pattern pieces on doubled flesh-coloured fabric, with the Head Front piece on a fold, as indicated. Align the Head Back piece with the grain of the fabric as shown above. Mark around each piece with a sharp pencil. This pencil line indicates the seams.

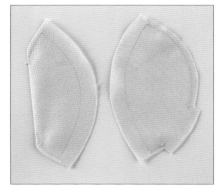

2 Machine stitch the centre-back seam of the Head Back leaving the 'opening' unstitched. Stitch the darts on the Head Front piece. Cut out these two pieces with a 6mm (¼in) seam allowance on the side seams and 3mm (⅛in) allowance on the darts and centre-back seam. Mark the side seams in pencil on both sides of the fabric.

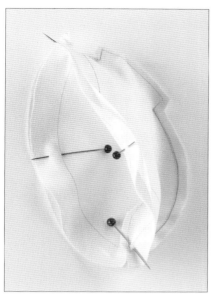

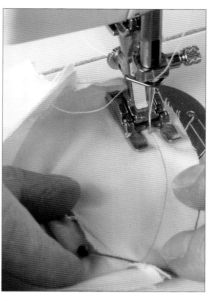

3 Pin together the front and back of the head, right sides together, matching the centre-back seam and the centre-front at the forehead and chin. Also match the sewing lines of the side seams.

4 Machine stitch around the side seam. You will now have a centre-back opening.

5 Trim the seams to approximately 3mm (⅛in) using a pair of small, sharp scissors.

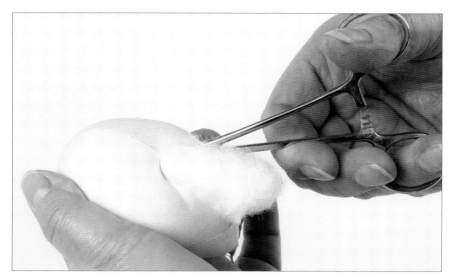

6 Pull through to the right side. Use either a chopstick or forceps to smooth around the seams inside the head to give a smooth finish when stuffed. Stuff the head firmly, making sure you have a nice smooth finish and a good shaped head.

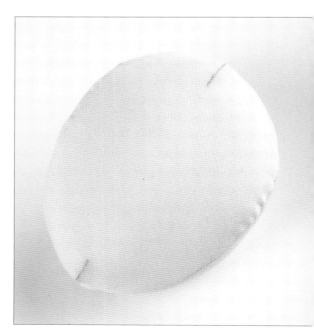

7 The finished head. Pin together the opening – we shall be putting the neck into this opening when the doll is almost complete.

Drawing and colouring the face

The positions of the features are first plotted on to the face using glass-headed pins. This needs to be done carefully and accurately to achieve a realistically proportioned face. The features are then drawn in with an air-vanishing fine-line pen. If you don't like what you have drawn it will vanish in a short while – use the pen lightly or the marks will take longer to disappear. Once you are happy with your doll's face, use the pens and watercolour crayons to colour the face permanently using either the colours specified or your own choice of colours. Blend the colours together by rubbing with a soft cloth or a cotton bud/swab for a more painterly effect.

YOU WILL NEED

Vanishing fine-line pen

Glass-headed pins

Micron Pigma pens (sizes 01 and 005) in black, brown and blue

Watercolour pencil crayons in dark and light blue, crimson, carmine red, burnt ochre, dark umber, yellow ochre, pink and white

White acrylic paint and a fine paintbrush

Cotton bud/swab or soft cloth

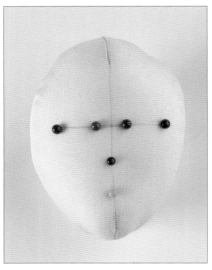

Positioning the features.

1 Begin by mapping out the positions of the features. Using a vanishing fine-line pen, lightly draw a vertical line between the two darts, then draw a horizontal line halfway down the face. Now you have a cross. Next insert pins as shown – evenly spaced on either side of the vertical line to represent the locations of the inner and outer corners of the eyes, and two more spaced evenly along the lower part of the vertical line to locate the centre of the lower part of the nose and the mouth.

2 Use the vanishing fine-line pen to draw the features on to the face (refer to the diagram, right). Position with dots the corners of the eyes and draw them in – first a circle, then the eyelid and then the iris and pupil. Next mark the position of the nostrils and then both corners of the mouth. Draw in the side flares and centre part of the nose, and the centre line of the mouth. Finally draw the upper and lower lip lines.

Tip

Before drawing the doll's face directly on to the head, I would recommend that you draw a few experimental faces on paper as well as a spare piece of fabric to get accustomed to how the pens and pencils behave.

3 Colour the face, following the instructions opposite. Spray lightly with artist's fixative spray, held 25–30cm (10–12in) away from the face.

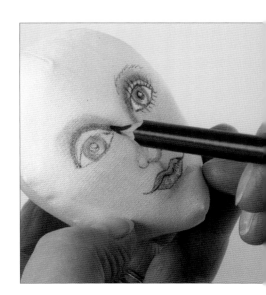

Colouring instructions

1 With the brown Micron Pigma pen draw over the three lines of the mouth and lightly fill in the nostrils.

2 With the black Micron Pigma pen draw over the lines for the eyes, eyelids and pupils. Fill in the pupils, leaving a white segment on the right-hand side for a highlight.

3 Outline the irises in the blue pen, though not the part underneath the eyelid.

Next you will add colour with the watercolour pencil crayons. You can blend the colours on the face with a small piece of soft cloth or a cotton bud/swab. Rub the larger areas of colour as you go and this will blend the colours together smoothly.

4 Fill in the irises using straight lines radiating outwards from the centre of the eye. Use a dark blue on the left-hand side and leave a white highlight on the opposite side, next to the highlight in the pupil. Gradually blend the dark blue into a lighter blue as you move around the eye towards the highlight. Do not colour the part of the iris underneath the eyelid.

5 Use both reds for the lips – colour the top lip with the crimson (the darker red) and the lower lip with the carmine red, which is lighter. Leave white highlights as indicated in the drawing on both the upper and the lower lip.

6 Shade the upper part of the eye sockets, just below the eyebrows, with burnt ochre, taking the colour down both sides of the nose.

7 Use dark umber around the lower part of the eye socket, leaving the eyelid free of colour, to recede the eye socket and give the face a three-dimensional appearance. Again, take the colour down the sides of the nose.

8 Use white watercolour crayon on the eyelids themselves, the dorsum (the ridge of the nose) and the forehead to highlight these areas.

9 With burnt ochre shade the tip of the nose and the outside of each nostril. Apply the colour in a circle around the outside and gradually fade it out as you work inwards, leaving a highlight in the middle. Also shade one side of the philtrum (the area just below the nose and above the top lip), around the chin and down each side of the face. Blend the colour carefully to get a smooth transition between the different areas of shading.

10 Colour under the eyes and the top part of the forehead with yellow ochre.

11 Shade the cheeks pink and blend in the colour.

12 With the black Micron Pigma pen draw in the eyebrows using lots of tiny strokes.

13 Draw in the top and bottom eyelashes with the same pen.

14 Use white acrylic to paint in the highlights on the irises, pupils and lips, and to fill the eye whites.

Colouring the face.

23

The completed face.

Needle-sculpted faces

Making the head

This is a four-part head – two pieces for the front and two pieces for the back, both cut double on the bias.

I always make a number of heads at a time and keep them in a bag. I often go back to them later and choose a head which matches a particular doll.

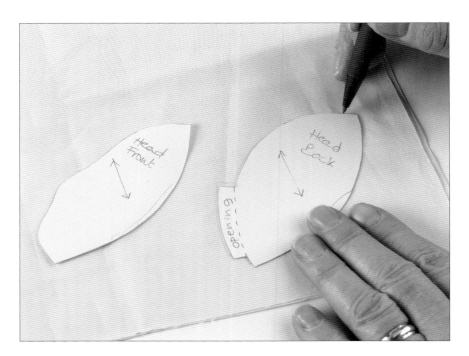

1 Place the template pieces on doubled fabric, aligned with the grain as shown left. Trace around the pieces carefully with a sharp pencil (remember, these lines are the stitching lines).

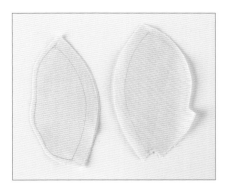

2 Machine stitch the centre-front and centre-back seams, leaving the back opening. Mark the sewing line in pencil on both sides of the fabric. Cut out the pieces with a 3mm (⅛in) seam allowance on the machined seams and 6mm (¼in) on the side seams.

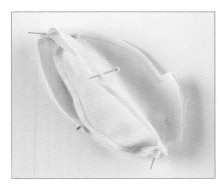

3 Pin together the back and front pieces of the head, matching the seams at the top and bottom and all the side seams. Machine together the side seams and trim to approximately 3mm (⅛in) using a pair of small, sharp scissors. Turn the head right-side out and use either a chopstick or forceps to smooth around the seams inside to give a smooth finish when stuffed.

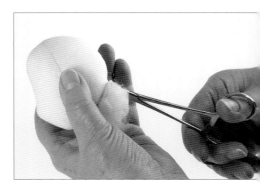

4 Stuff the head firmly and evenly, making sure the stuffing goes into the nose. When you think the head is stuffed sufficiently, close the opening with pins. Leave enough space to insert the neck when you are ready to attach the head to the body. You are now ready to do the sculpting.

Needle-sculpting the face

To needle-sculpt the face, follow the steps below. The sculpting stitches need to be pulled firmly to form the face shape, but not too tightly.

When first starting to needle-sculpt dolls' faces, you might find it helpful to make two or three and use the best one. It gives practice in making, and if one goes wrong there are still two more to choose from!

YOU WILL NEED

Long, fine darning needle

Quilting thread in colour to match fabric (natural is generally a good match)

Glass-headed pins

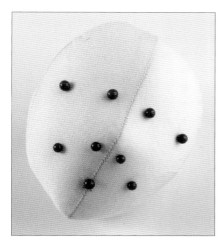

1 Mark the positions of the features with pins. This will help with the proportions of the face. Place two pins approximately 1.5cm (³⁄₄in) apart on either side of the centre-front seam to mark the inner and outer corners of the eyes. Place two pins just below the tip of the nose for the nostrils and three below these marking the corners and middle of the mouth.

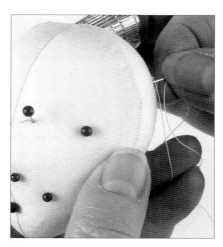

2 Thread a long, fine darning needle with about 1m (39½in) of quilting thread, and secure the thread at the back of the head with a couple of stitches. Push the needle through the head and out at the inner right-hand pin.

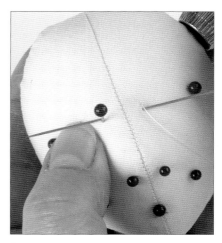

3 Remove the pin and make a small stitch by putting the needle back in as close as possible to where it came through, and take it across to the inner left-hand pin.

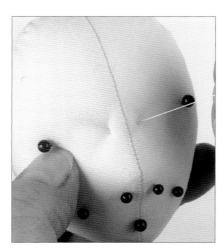

4 Pull the thread taut then repeat, making a small stitch on the left-hand side of the nose and taking the thread back across to the first stitch on the right. This forms the bridge of the nose. Repeat two or three times.

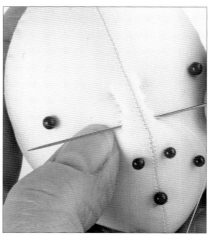

5 Continue down the nose, stopping on the left-hand side just before you reach the tip. With each stitch, manipulate the stuffing into the nose with your needle or fingers.

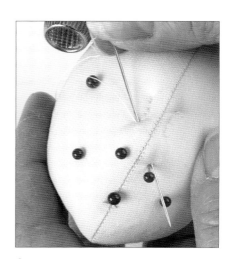

6 Take the needle across from the left-hand side of the nose and bring it out through the right-hand nostril.

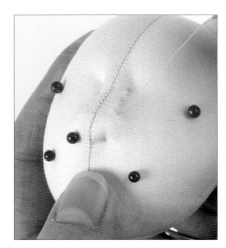

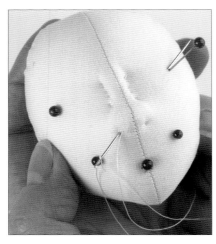

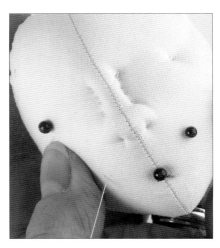

7 Pass the needle back through the nostril and bring it out through the lower right-hand part of the nose. Pull the thread taut.

8 Take the thread across and bring it out through the left-hand nostril, then make a small stitch and take the needle across to the furthest right-hand pin. Remember to remove the pins as you go.

9 Make a tiny stitch at the outer corner of the eye, and take the thread right across to the left-hand corner of the mouth.

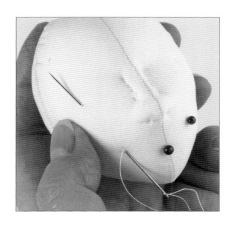

Tip

Remember that the sculpting stitches need to be pulled firmly to form the face shape, but not too tightly. Remove the pins as you go, leaving only the lower pin in the centre of the mouth in place at the end.

10 Make a small stitch and take the thread up to the outer corner of the left-hand eye.

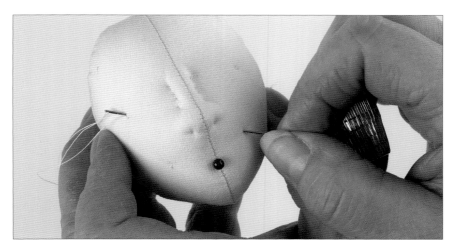

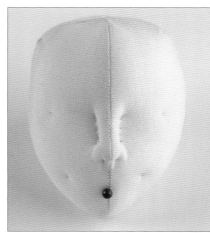

11 Pass the needle back through to form a small stitch and bring it out at the right-hand corner of the mouth.

12 To finish, take the thread through to the back of the head and fasten off. Leave the pin marking the centre of the mouth in place.

Colouring the face

This is very similar to drawing and colouring the flat face. In fact, plotting the features is now made simpler as the needle-sculpting defines their positions. I used different coloured pens and crayons for this doll; use any colours you choose.

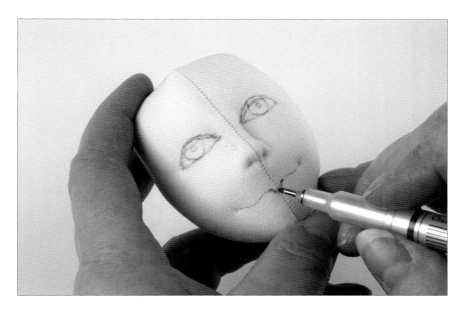

1 Begin by marking out the features with a vanishing fine-line pen, using the needle-sculpting to get the position and size of the features correct. This face is very simple and as long as you get the features properly positioned to start with it is actually quite easy to get a successful result (see below).

Positioning the features.

2 When all of the doll's features are marked in with vanishing fine-line pen, the face is ready for painting.

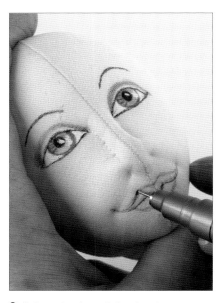

3 Colour the face, following the instructions on the following page. Put to one side, ready for use.

Tip

Use artist's fixative spray to fix the face after it has been coloured. Spray lightly from a distance of 25–30cm (10–12in).

Colouring instructions

1 With the brown Micron Pigma pen draw over the three lines of the mouth and lightly fill in the nostrils.

2 With the black Micron Pigma pen draw over the lines for the eyes, eyelids and pupils. Fill in the pupils, leaving a white segment on the right-hand side for a highlight.

3 Outline each iris in the green pen. Do not outline the part of the iris underneath the eyelid.

Next you will add colour with the watercolour pencil crayons. You can blend the colours on the face with a small piece of soft cloth or a cotton bud/swab. Rub the larger areas of colour as you go and this will blend the colours together smoothly.

4 Fill in the irises using straight lines radiating outwards from the centre of the eye. Use a dark green on the left-hand side and leave a white highlight on the opposite side, next to the highlight in the pupil. Gradually blend the dark green into a lighter green as you move around the eye towards the highlight. Do not colour the part of the iris underneath the eyelid.

5 Use process red and magenta for the lips. Colour the top lip darker than the lower lip. Leave white highlights as indicated in the drawing.

6 Shade the upper part of the eye sockets, just below the eyebrows, with light umber, taking the colour down both sides of the nose.

7 Use grape to colour the lower part of the eye socket, leaving the eyelid free of colour, to recede the eye socket and give the face a three-dimensional appearance. Take this down the side of the nose also.

8 Use white watercolour crayon on the eyelids themselves, the dorsum (the ridge of the nose) and the forehead to highlight these areas.

9 With light umber shade the tip of the nose and the outside of each nostril. Apply the colour in a circle around the outside and gradually fade it out as you work inwards, leaving a highlight in the middle. Also shade one side of the philtrum (the area just below the nose and above the top lip), around the chin, across the top of the forehead and down each side of the face. Blend the colour carefully to get a smooth transition between the different areas of shading.

10 Colour under the eyes and the forehead with yellow ochre. Take the yellow ochre down the top of the nose.

11 Shade the cheeks pink and blend in the colour.

12 With the black Micron Pigma pen draw in the eyebrows using either lots of tiny strokes or a single thick line.

13 Lastly draw in the top and bottom eyelashes with the same pen – longer lashes along the top lid and shorter along the bottom.

14 Use white acrylic to paint in the highlights on the irises, pupils and lips, and to fill the eye whites.

The completed face.

Attaching the head to the body

YOU WILL NEED

Chopstick or 12cm (5in) forceps

Glass-headed pins

Quilting thread in colour to match fabric

Long, fine darning needle

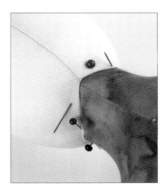

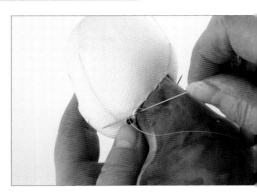

1 Take your finished head and remove the pin holding the back opening closed. With forceps or a chopstick push a space into the back of the head. Using the forceps push the neck of the body into the space made in the head. Make sure the head is the right way round and straight.

2 Hold the head in place securely and pin, turning in the edges of the head opening neatly.

3 Ladder stitch the head in place using quilting thread and a long, fine darning needle (see pages 42–43).

Making ears

Depending on the style of your doll, you may not need to make ears if they will be hidden underneath the doll's hair. Some fantasy dolls, however, for example fairies, elves and mermaids, have large, prominent, pointed ears, for which I have provided templates.

YOU WILL NEED

Flesh-coloured fabric and matching sewing thread

Template (see page 131)

Sharp pencil or mechanical pencil

Small, sharp scissors

Vanishing fine-line pen

Tweezers or 12cm (5in) forceps

Handful of stuffing

Long, fine darning needle, size 7

29

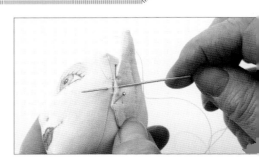

1 On doubled fabric, draw around the ear template twice. Machine stitch around each ear on the line, leaving the opening. Cut out each ear with a 3mm (⅛in) seam allowance.

2 Pull the ears the right way out using the tweezers or forceps. Fill them with a little stuffing to pad them out, but avoid over-filling. Turn in the edges of the openings and stitch them closed.

3 Topstitch lines on to each ear to give them character and form. You may like to draw these on first with a vanishing fine-line pen. Make sure the ears are mirror images of each other.

4 Pin an ear on to each side of the head, laying the stitched opening along the side seam and aligning the top of it with the eyes. Stitch the ears in place.

Making hands

This section covers three types of hands: mitt hands with a thumb; a simple hand with the three centre fingers made as one piece and topstitched on the right side; and five-fingered hands including a thumb. All have wired fingers and are slightly stuffed to give some shape to the hands, allowing you to make a pair of hands for each doll. Make sure you have one right hand and one left hand. For templates, see pages 129, 131 and 134.

Mitt hands

A good choice for a cloth doll is a mitt hand, which has a separate thumb and stab-stitched fingers wired with chenille sticks (pipe cleaners). This means they can be bent into position on the doll.

YOU WILL NEED

Flesh-coloured fabric and matching sewing thread

Template (see page 129)

Sharp pencil or mechanical pencil

Glass-headed pins

Small, sharp scissors

Vanishing fine-line pen

Tweezers or 12cm (5in) forceps

Three 30cm (12in) long chenille sticks (pipe cleaners), 6 or 9mm

Handful of stuffing

Long, fine darning needle, size 7

Quilting thread in colour to match fabric

Seam sealant (or PVA glue)

1 Draw around the hand and arm template on to doubled flesh-coloured fabric using a sharp pencil. Using a small stitch size (1–2), machine stitch on the line leaving the ends of the arms open.

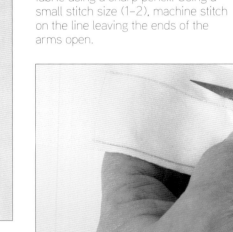

2 With the small scissors trim around the seams leaving a 3mm (⅛in) allowance. Do not trim the fabric between the thumb and the hand at this stage.

3 Put a dab of seam sealant on both sides of the fabric between the thumb and the hand and allow to dry. With small, sharp scissors snip down between the thumb and the hand. Get as close as possible to the stitches of the seam, being careful not to snip through them. If you don't snip close enough to the seam you will end up with wrinkles around the thumb when you pull the hand through. Trim away some of the excess fabric between the thumb and hand, then pull the hand through to the right side with forceps.

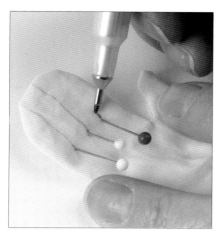

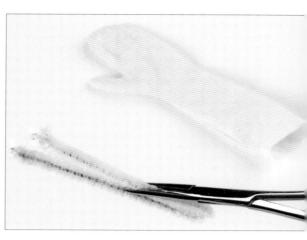

4 Mark the bases of the fingers with pins and draw in the fingers using a vanishing fine-line pen.

5 Remove the pins and machine stitch down the sides of the fingers. Fasten off at the base of each one.

6 Insert chenille sticks into the fingers and thumb to give them body and shape. Cut three chenille sticks in half and turn down the sharp ends with your forceps. Bend all six pieces in half again.

7 Using the forceps, push one folded chenille stick into the first two fingers of one hand (one half of the folded stick into each finger) and repeat for the next two fingers. Do this for both hands.

8 You now have two folded pieces of chenille stick left. Insert one into the thumb of each hand with the 'bend' going in first. Twist all the ends together at the wrist.

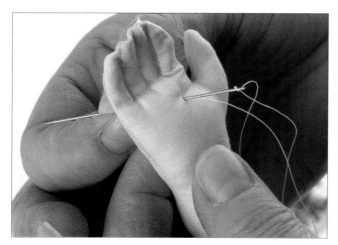

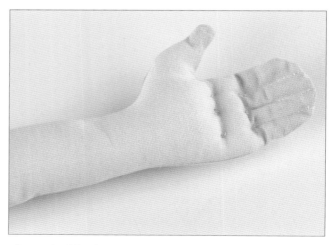

9 Stuff the palm of each hand, creating a right and left hand. Put two or three stab stitches near the base of each finger and across the palm to give the hand a more realistic form. Now you can bend the hand into a natural shape.

The completed hand.

Simple hand

These hands have the little finger and thumb as separate digits with the three centre fingers made in one piece and then topstitched on the right side.

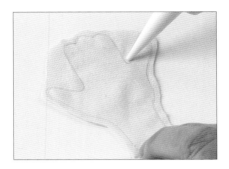

1 Place the hand template on doubled fabric and draw around it very carefully with a pencil. Repeat to make two hands. Starting at the wrist, machine stitch on the pencil lines as accurately as you can, making sure there are at least two stitches between the thumb and the middle fingers and between the little finger and the middle fingers. Leave the wrist open. Cut out each hand with a 3mm (⅛in) seam allowance, but for now leave fabric between the middle three fingers and the thumb and little finger, as shown.

2 Put a dab of seam sealant on to both sides of the fabric between the thumb and the middle fingers, and between the little finger and the middle fingers. Do this on both hands and allow to dry.

3 With small, sharp scissors, cut down between the thumb and the middle three fingers almost to the seam. Trim back the excess fabric to approximately 3mm (⅛in). Trim the fabric between the little finger and the middle fingers in the same way. Repeat for both hands.

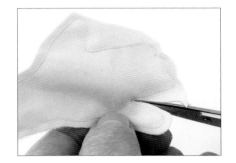

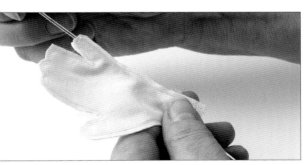

4 Turn each hand the right way out. Use finger-turning tools for the thumb and little finger. Insert the tube in the finger and position the rod at the top. Push the fabric up over the rod, pressing the tube against your body to keep it stable. If you don't have any finger-turning tools, ease out the thumb and little finger by pushing and pulling the fabric with the forceps then ease out the end using a darning needle. For the middle three fingers, use the forceps to pull the fabric through.

5 Mark on the three middle fingers using a vanishing fine-line pen. Mark the ends of the lines with pins if necessary. Run a line of machine stitching along each line.

6 Wire each hand in the same way. First cut three 30cm (12in) chenille sticks in half and fold each one in half again. This will give you six folded lengths of chenille stick – three for each hand. Bend down the ends using a pair of forceps. With the forceps, insert the two ends of one folded chenille stick into the two middle fingers nearest the thumb. Repeat for the third middle finger and the little finger.

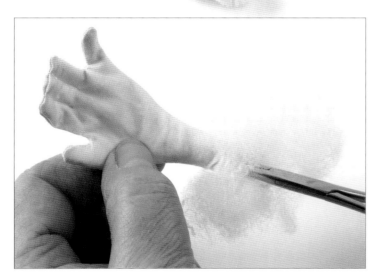

7 For the thumb, push in a third folded chenille stick with the bend going in first. Twist all the chenille sticks together at the wrist. Manipulate the fingers into a life-like position.

8 Put a little stuffing into the palm of the hand and a little less stuffing into the back of the hand. Make a left and a right hand.

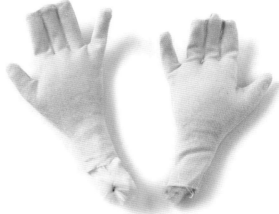

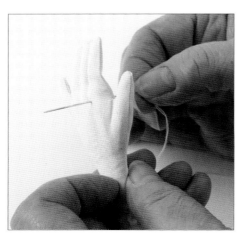

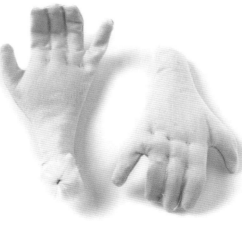

9 Add some sculpting stitches to make the knuckles; work two or three tiny stitches where each pair of fingers join at the base.

Five-fingered hands

Hands with separate fingers are more awkward to make and may need some practice to achieve, but the results are rewarding. They are also wired with chenille sticks and can therefore be posed. Some colour can be added and nails drawn on after they are made.

YOU WILL NEED

Flesh-coloured fabric and matching sewing thread

Template (see page 134)

Sharp pencil or mechanical pencil

Small, sharp scissors

Tweezers or 12cm (5in) forceps

Finger-turning tools

Three 30cm (12in) long chenille sticks (pipe cleaners), 6 or 9mm

Long, fine darning needle, size 7

Quilting thread in colour to match fabric

Seam sealant (or PVA glue)

Small amount of stuffing

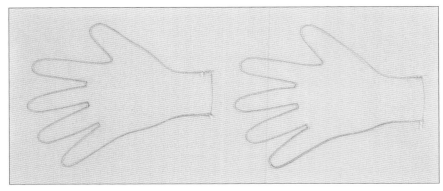

1 Using the template provided, draw the outlines for the hands on to doubled fabric using a sharp pencil. Using a stitch size 1–2, machine stitch around the hand leaving the wrist open. Make sure you have two stitches between each finger to enable successful turning.

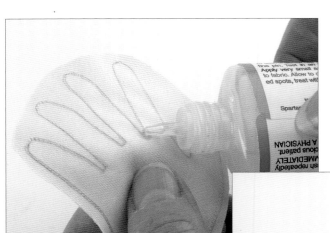

2 Cut around each hand using a pair of small, sharp scissors, but do not cut in between the individual fingers. Trim the seams to 3mm (⅛in). Put a dab of seam sealant or PVA glue on to the fabric between each finger on both sides.

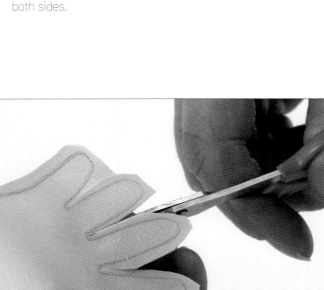

3 Allow to dry, then snip to the seam between each finger. The closer to the seam you cut the better the fingers will look, but take care not to snip through the stitches.

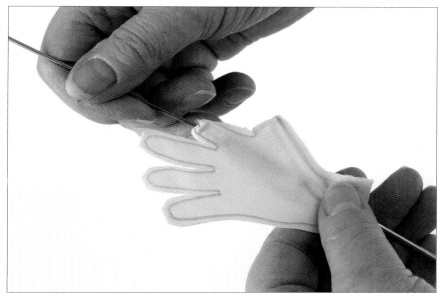

4 Turn each finger individually using the finger-turning tools. Put a tube into a finger and hold it in place by placing the rod slightly into the top of the tube. Push the fabric of the finger up over the rod. This will take a little time and patience.

5 When all the fingers are turned pull the hand through with your forceps.

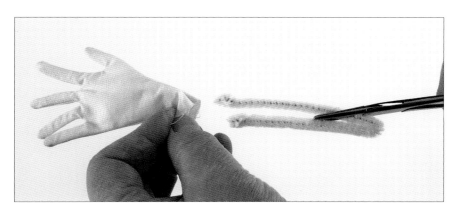

6 Cut all three chenille sticks in half, turn down the ends using the forceps so they are blunt and fold them in half. Use the forceps to insert one folded chenille stick into the first two fingers, pushing one half of the stick into each finger.

7 Repeat for the other two fingers. Push both halves of a folded chenille stick into the thumb, with the 'bend' inserted first. Repeat for the other hand.

8 Twist all the chenille sticks together at the wrist.

9 Put a little stuffing into the palm of the hand with forceps and put in a few small sculpting stitches to form the knuckles and wrist, giving the hand a little more shape.

Tip

Make sure you make a left and a right hand.

Making feet

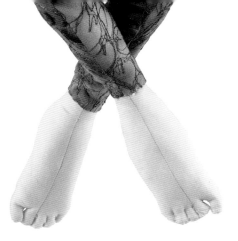

A foot can be a simple shape made as part of the leg, or it can be further developed and made separately, with individual toes stab-stitched in after the foot is turned, and inserted into the leg at the ankle. The template can be found on page 134.

Making separate feet

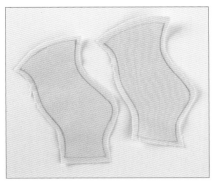

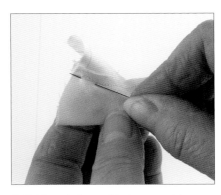

36

1 Mark the template for the foot on to doubled flesh-coloured fabric twice and machine stitch along the side seams using stitch size 1–2. Cut each one out, leaving a seam allowance of 3mm (⅛in).

2 Fold each foot with the two side seams together and pin in place.

Tip

Remember to make a left and a right foot.

3 Use the vanishing fine-line pen to draw in the shape of the toes – a single curve for the four small toes and a separate big toe.

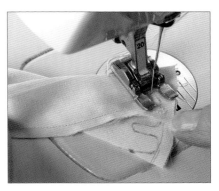

4 Machine stitch along the drawn line.

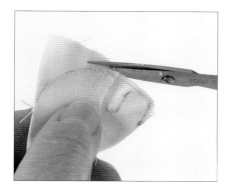

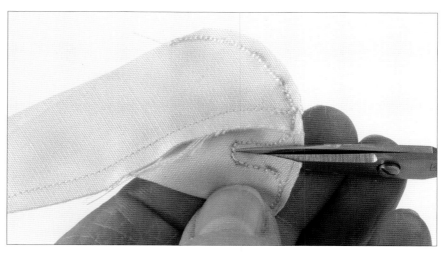

5 Use a pair of small, sharp scissors to trim around the ends of the toes, leaving a narrow seam allowance of about 3mm (⅛in). Add a dab of seam sealant between the big toe and the rest of the foot.

6 Snip down in between the big toe and the rest of the foot. Snip down as close as possible to the seam but without cutting through the stitching.

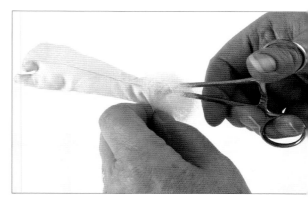

7 Use the forceps to pull the foot through to the right side.

8 Stuff the foot firmly using the forceps, pushing the stuffing into the big toe.

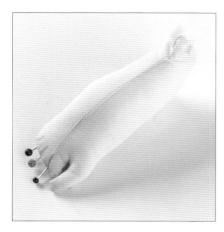

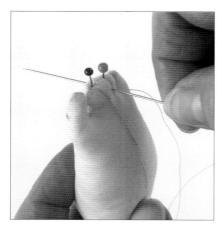

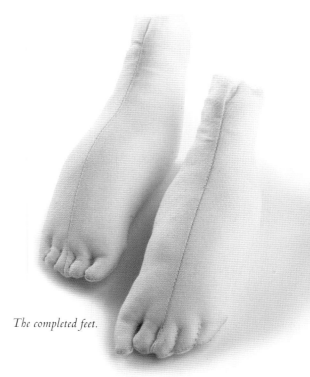

9 Mark the positions of the four small toes with pins inserted into the end of the foot, and draw in the toes using the vanishing fine-line pen.

10 Stab stitch along the lines using a long, fine darning needle and quilting thread. Start at the base of each toe, and when you reach the end stitch over the top of the toe and pull the thread taut to shape it.

The completed feet.

PROJECTS

This book contains six different step-by-step projects. Each doll can be customized by following the same set of instructions but changing the colours, fabrics and trims. I have therefore included an alternative design at the end of each project, which shows you how a very different looking doll can be made by using the same templates and instructions. A great deal of fun can be had designing the dolls' costumes and experimenting with different colouring mediums, fabrics and embellishments.

If you are new to cloth-doll making, try out the techniques first and make sure you have all of the equipment and materials you need to get started. The methods for making the heads, faces, hands and feet are all detailed in the previous sections of the book and you should refer back to these. All the templates are provided at the back of the book and are interchangeable from doll to doll as they are all made to the same scale.

Before you start ...

Remember that the lines on the templates are the sewing lines, to which you need to add a seam allowance. The seam allowance for a stitched seam is 3mm (⅛in) and for a seam to be sewn after cutting the allowance is 6mm (¼in). In most cases you will trace the templates on to doubled fabric with a mechanical pencil, machine stitch along the pattern line and then cut out. There are specific instructions with each project where this may vary. Use the open appliqué foot on your sewing machine and a small stitch size (about 1–2, depending upon the type of machine). This enables you to stitch around small pieces and also makes a strong seam.

Miranda

This is a simple doll to make, with a flat face and mitt hands. She is fully jointed with stitched joints. Either follow the colour scheme shown here, or choose your own colour scheme from your fabric stash. Lay out all your suitable fabric pieces and trims to make your selection. You will probably find that you will change your mind as you put the doll together, but you need an initial 'colour story' to begin.

Head

1 Make the head and colour the face following the instructions for a flat face on pages 20–23. Hold the opening for the neck closed with pins. Put to one side while you make the rest of the doll.

YOU WILL NEED

Templates (pages 128–129)

Flesh-coloured cotton fabric: 25cm (¼yd)

Woven cotton or dupion silk fabric: 10 x 30cm (4 x 12in) dark orange for sleeves, 25cm (¼yd) cerise for body, 25cm (¼yd) blue for legs

Polyester tulle in yellow and red: 50cm (½yd) of each colour

Silver net: 25cm (¼yd)

Multi-coloured dyed habotai silk: 50cm (½yd)

7mm (¼in) satin ribbon in red and purple: 2m (80in) of each colour

Striped or painted ribbon for bodice trim: 45cm (18in)

Small 6mm (¼in) buttons or beads for trims

Two balls of fancy yarns for hair

Four 15mm (½in) two-hole buttons for jointing

Sewing machine with open-toe quilting foot and new needle

Three 30cm (12in), 6mm (¼in) chenille sticks (pipe cleaners)

250g (½lb) bag of polyester stuffing

Extra-strong upholstery thread for jointing

Quilting thread for closing seams after stuffing

Basic sewing kit of sewing needles, scissors, pins, 12cm (5in) forceps or hemostats and polyester threads in a variety of colours to match the fabrics used

Long doll needles for jointing

Long, fine darning needle, size 7

Chopstick or stuffing tool

Sharp pencil or mechanical pencil

Vanishing fine-line pen

Seam sealant (or PVA glue)

Face-colouring equipment (see pages 16–17)

Ruler

Body

The body is made from a piece of flesh-coloured cotton for the top section and plain cerise silk for the lower part. Pay particular attention to the neck, shoulders and hips when stuffing as these parts take the strain of jointing and holding the head and need to be strong.

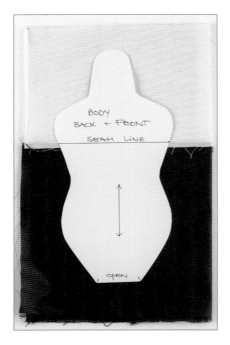

2 Prepare a piece of flesh-coloured cotton 30 x 10cm (11¾ x 4in) and a piece of cerise silk 30 x 15cm (11¾ x 6in). The grain should run with the 10cm (4in) and 15cm (6in) sides. Seam the two pieces together along the 30cm (11¾in) side. Press the seam on to the silk side so that it does not show through the flesh-coloured section. Fold this piece in half with the seam horizontal and the right sides together. Place the template for the body piece on to the fabric, with the horizontal dashed line on the template on the seam line of the fabric.

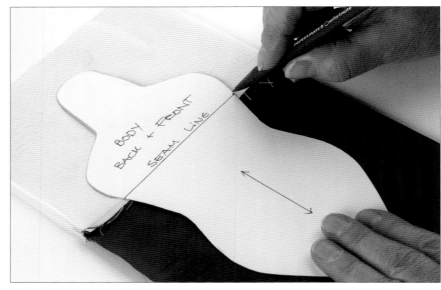

3 Trace all round this pattern with a sharp pencil.

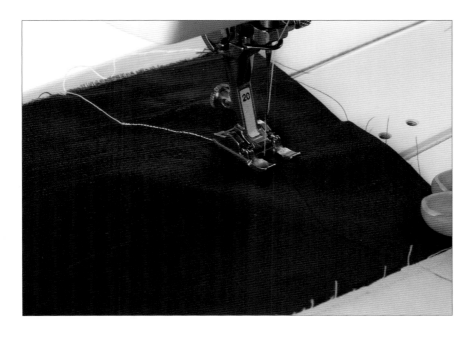

4 Machine stitch around the body on the pencil line, but leave the opening at the bottom of the body as marked on the pattern. Use flesh-coloured thread and small (size 1–2) stitches.

Ladder stitch

This stitch is used to close the openings in seams after stuffing a piece. Use a normal sewing needle and some polyester thread in a colour that matches the fabric. Fasten the thread at the beginning of the opening, then go in at 1 and out at 2, etc., as in the diagram. Pull the thread taut every few stitches and the opening will close up invisibly.

5 Cut out the body with a 3mm (⅛in) seam allowance. Make the allowance for the opening 6mm (¼in) as it needs to be turned in after stuffing. Do not clip the seams.

6 Turn the body the right way out and stuff (see page 19). Take a good handful of stuffing and start to fill the neck first, then fill the body cavity. Push the stuffing into the shoulders and hips to make them very firm. This is important as they must be strong enough to hold the jointing of the limbs. If the body is too soft the arms and legs will not sit properly when jointed on. When you are satisfied with the stuffing, close the opening by pushing in the seam allowance and hold it in place with pins before ladder stitching (see below).

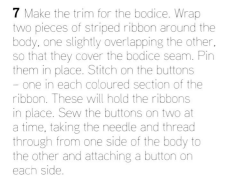

7 Make the trim for the bodice. Wrap two pieces of striped ribbon around the body, one slightly overlapping the other, so that they cover the bodice seam. Pin them in place. Stitch on the buttons – one in each coloured section of the ribbon. These will hold the ribbons in place. Sew the buttons on two at a time, taking the needle and thread through from one side of the body to the other and attaching a button on each side.

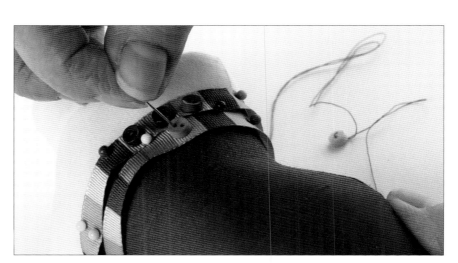

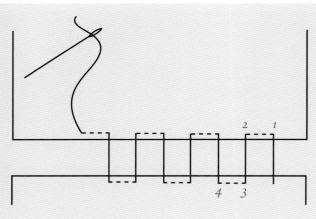

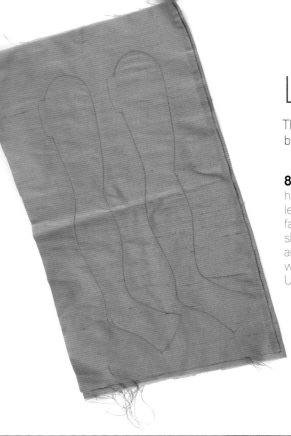

Legs

These are both made the same, from a piece of bright blue dupion silk.

8 Take the fabric for the legs and fold it in half, right sides together, with the grain running lengthways. Trace two legs on to this doubled fabric, with the joint lines marked on, using a sharp pencil. With a matching thread, machine around the outlines leaving the foot open as well as the opening at the top of the thigh. Use small stitches.

9 Cut out the legs with a 3mm (⅛in) seam allowance. Re-fold each foot with the back and front seams on top of one another and draw a neat, rounded shape on to each foot using a sharp pencil. Machine stitch along this line and trim the seam around each foot to 3mm (⅛in).

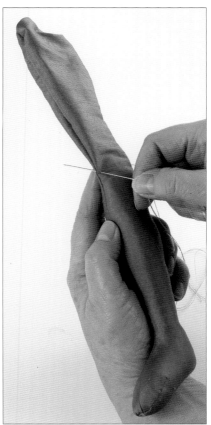

10 Turn each leg right-side out and smooth the seams on the inside, especially around the foot. Stuff the foot and ankle firmly, using the forceps to get the stuffing right into the toe. Make sure the ankle is very firm. Stuff the leg up to 1cm (½in) below the knee joint mark. Make the knee joint following the instructions in the box opposite. Because you did not stuff right up to the knee joint, the lower leg can move freely.

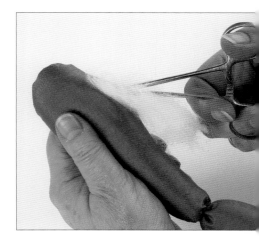

11 Stuff the remainder of the leg firmly. Tuck in the seam allowance at the opening and close it with ladder stitch (see pages 42–43).

Making a knee joint or elbow

Take a length of doubled polyester thread in a colour that matches the fabric and a hand-sewing needle. Join the thread to the seam at the back of the leg with a couple of stitches (1). Next, take the thread through the leg to the front and make a small stitch, then take the thread round the leg and make another stitch at the back (2). Pull the thread tight to form the joint. Wind the thread tightly around the joint two or three times and finish off securely (3).

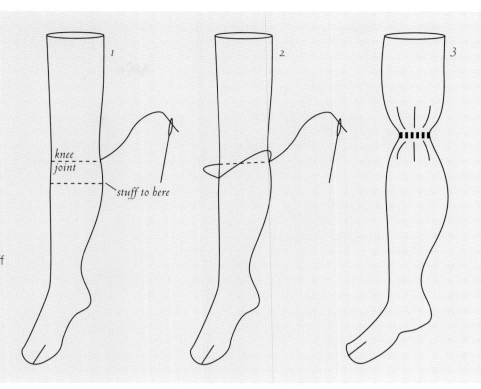

Arms and hands

Like the body, the arms are made from two pieces of fabric stitched together – dark orange at the top to make the sleeves, and flesh-coloured at the bottom for the lower arms.

12 Start by joining two fabric pieces together, as for the body (see page 42). You will need a piece of flesh-coloured cotton 30 x 15cm (12 x 6in) and a piece of dark orange silk, 30 x 10cm (12 x 4in) for the top of the arm. The grain should run along the shorter sides. Seam together the 30cm (12in) sides and press the seam down so that it lays over the coloured fabric. Fold the fabric piece in half with the seam horizontal and the right sides together. Place the template for the arm on the fabric, with the horizontal line on the template aligned with the seam. Leave enough room for a second arm to be positioned alongside it. Draw around the template using a sharp pencil, then transfer a second arm in the same way. Machine stitch around both arms using flesh-coloured thread, leaving the opening.

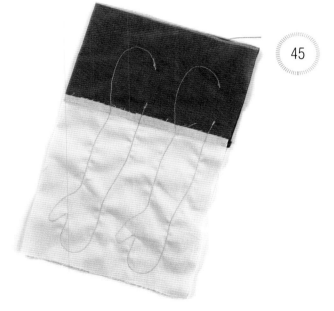

13 Cut out both arms with a 3mm (⅛in) seam allowance. Leave a little more around the opening flap. Make the hands following the instructions for mitt hands on pages 30–31. Stuff the lower part of each arm. Push the stuffing into the hand and wrist first and make sure they are shaped nicely. Put more stuffing into the palm of each hand, ensuring you make a left and a right hand. Fill the lower arm to 1cm (½in) below the seam line.

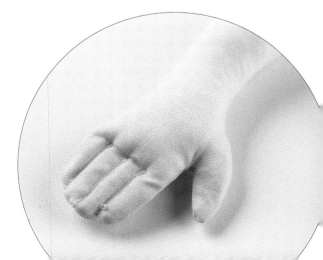

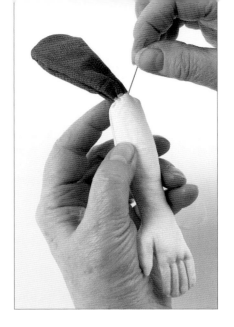

14 Make the elbow joint on the seam line where the two fabrics are joined, following the instructions in the box on page 45. Because you did not stuff right up to the seam the arm can move freely. Finish stuffing the upper arm, close the opening and push the turnings well in. Ladder stitch to close (see pages 42–43).

Jointing the legs to the body

You will need two 15mm (¾in) buttons, a long doll needle for jointing and about 1m (40in) of extra-strong upholstery thread. The legs are button jointed to the body on either side of the hips.

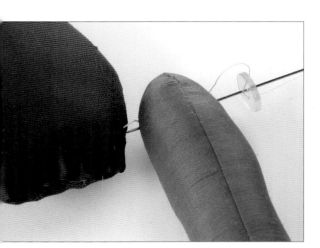

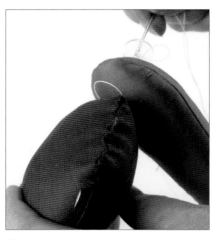

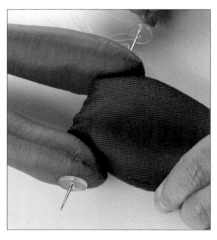

15 Attach the thread to one hip of the doll's body with two or three small stitches. Push the needle through the top of the leg and then the button, then back through the button and the leg to the body.

16 Continue to push the needle through the lower part of the body, coming out in the same position on the other hip.

17 Take the needle through the other leg, button and back again. Pull this thread to keep a firm tension but take care not to snap the thread.

18 Repeat two or three times and fasten off.

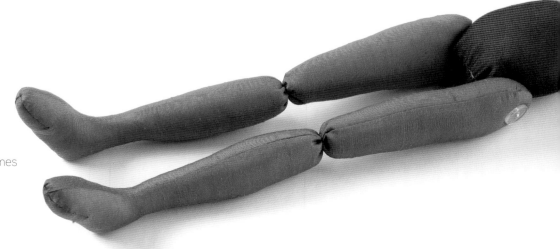

Jointing the arms to the body

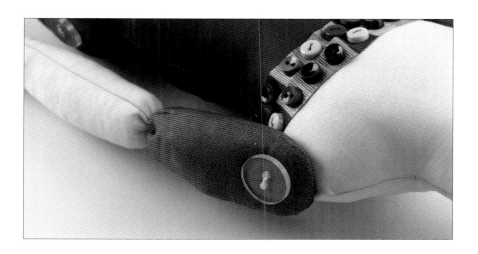

19 The arms are button jointed to the body in the same way as the legs. Attach them to the sides of the body, so that the tops of the arms are level with the shoulders.

Attaching the head

20 Attach the head to the body firmly (see page 29). Remove the pins from the opening at the back. Using forceps or a chopstick, make a good space in the back of the head. Push the neck into the head so that the face is nicely positioned. Pin it in place and ladder stitch securely. Your doll is now ready to dress.

Skirt

The skirt is made from four layers of polyester tulle in two colours – three layers of yellow and a single layer of red. You could use more colours than this, or just one colour – the choice is yours. Each layer of tulle measures 90 x 15cm (36 x 6in).

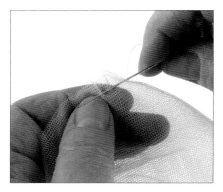

21 Run a line of gathering stitches along the top edge of each piece of tulle and pull up to fit around the doll's hips.

22 Wrap the first layer of tulle around the doll's hips, overlapping the two sides at the back. Tie the two ends of the gathering thread together to secure and pin in place if necessary. Use the same thread to stitch the skirt in place, following the line of gathering stitches.

23 Attach the other two layers of yellow tulle in the same way, followed by the red layer.

24 Take a piece of multi-coloured dyed habotai silk measuring 90 x 35cm (36 x 14in). Tear off two strips each 90cm (36in) long and 5cm (2in) wide for the sleeve trim and set aside. Fold the remaining 25cm (10in) strip in half lengthways. Hold the two long edges together by running a gathering thread along them. Pull up the gathering thread and fit the silk on to the doll's hips, just above the tulle. Pin it in place and stitch firmly.

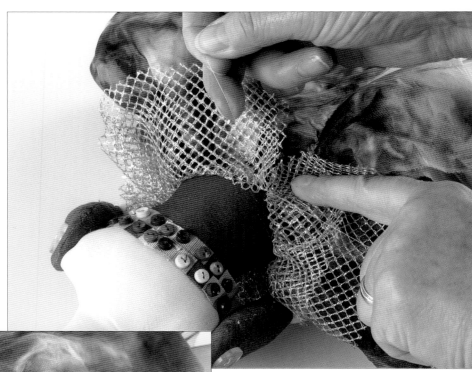

25 The last layer is made from silver net. This is a strip measuring 50 x 8cm (20 x 3in). Fold the net in half lengthways and gather it along the folded edge on to the doll's hips, as with the previous layers. Stitch it firmly in place.

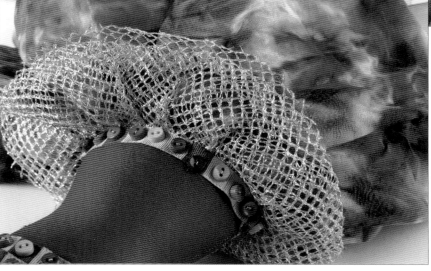

26 Pin a single strip of the striped ribbon over the top edge of the net and stitch it in place. Sew on buttons to match the bodice trim, passing the thread right through the body to attach a button on either side as before.

Frills around the arms and shoulders

There are two silk frills that go around the elbows made with the pieces retained from the skirt, and two frills in each colour of tulle. Two of these go around the elbows with the silk and two around the shoulder joint.

27 Cut two strips of red tulle 5cm (2in) wide. Fold each strip in half along its length so that it is 2.5cm (1in) deep and stitch the two long edges together by running a gathering thread along them. For each strip, pull the thread to gather the tulle into a frill and fit it between the arm and the shoulder. Pull the thread tight and tie it in a knot under the arm to secure. Trim off the ends of the thread.

28 Cut two strips of yellow tulle the same size as the red ones in step 27, and fold and gather them in the same way. Fit one yellow strip around each elbow to hide the stitching on the arm, pull the gathering thread tight and tie it in a knot. Use the same thread to secure the frill with two or three small stitches if necessary. Take the two strips of habotai silk you put by earlier, fold each one in half lengthways and again run a gathering thread along the two cut edges. For each one, pull up the thread to create a frill and place it around the elbow below the yellow one. Secure with a knot and two or three stitches if needed.

Hair

For the hair I have combined two types of fancy yarn in bright reds, yellows, pinks, oranges, purples and blues. The yarns I have chosen are a soft, bobbly, chenille-type yarn and a feathery eyelash yarn.

29 Take the ends of both balls of yarn and wind them around a book or DVD case to make a loose hank of mixed yarn about 25cm (10in) long. Spread this to around 6cm (2¼in) in width.

30 Cut through one side of the hank using a large pair of sharp scissors.

31 Machine stitch across the middle of the hank two or three times using large stitches.

32 Place the hair on the top of the head with the stitched line in the centre running front to back as a parting. Pin and then stitch the hair in place with a few holding stitches.

33 Trim the top layers of the hair using a large pair of sharp scissors to give it a more rounded shape.

Finishing touches

34 Cut a strip of silver net and another of red tulle and tie them each in a bow around the doll's head. Take a length of thin purple ribbon and tie it around her neck, securing it at the back with a few tiny stitches.

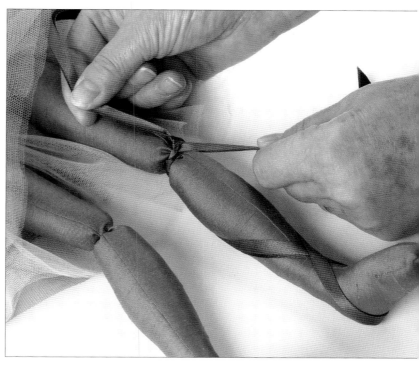

35 Take two lengths of each colour ribbon 70cm (28in) long. Holding two lengths – one of each colour – together, place the centre of the ribbons under one of the doll's feet, criss cross them at the ankle and take them round the back of the leg up to the knee. Tie them at the knee and catch with a stitch and a small button to secure.

36 Decorate the other leg in the same way. Trim the ribbons leaving long tails and sew on some tiny buttons to hold the ribbons in place at the ankle.

Bluebelle

This alternative version is made from the same templates and instructions but the fabrics, yarns and ribbons have been changed to create a more subtle, predominantly blue colour scheme. The bodice has been made from a printed cotton. The silver net is omitted and the dyed habotai silk is replaced by patterned tulle in turquoise.

Peaseblossom

Peaseblossom is a flower fairy with button-jointed hips and shoulders, and limbs with stitched joints. Her feet and hands are made separately and her body is shaped. Her wings are wired and made from heated organza, and her hair is Tibetan lamb skin coloured with fabric dye. She is decorated with organza flowers.

YOU WILL NEED

Templates (pages 130–132)

Fat quarter of flesh-coloured cotton fabric for the head, neck, hands and feet

Fat quarter of flower-printed cotton fabric for the body

Fat quarter of cotton batik fabric for the arms

Fat quarter of striped cotton fabric for the legs

50cm (½yd) of synthetic organza in two different colours for the skirt

250g (8oz) of polyester stuffing

15 x 15cm (6 x 6in) of bleached Tibetan lamb skin for the hair

Four 14mm (½in) buttons for jointing

Assorted 4mm (³/₁₆in) beads

Three 1m (1yd) lengths of synthetic organza in different colours for the wings, skirt and flowers

5m (5yd) of wired designer cord in a toning colour for the wings

Angelina fibres

Three 30cm (12in), 6mm (¼in) chenille sticks (pipe cleaners)

Sewing machine with open-toe quilting foot and new needle

Extra-strong thread in Natural for jointing

Quilting thread in Natural for sculpting

Basic sewing kit of sewing needle, scissors, pins, 12cm (5in) forceps or hemostats and polyester threads in a variety of colours to match the fabrics used

Long no. 7 darning needle and long doll needle

Fabric dye in red, violet and turquoise

Vanishing fine-line pen

Face colouring equipment (see pages 16–17)

Finger-turning tools (optional)

Mechanical or sharp HB pencil

Stuffing tools or chopstick

Heat gun

Glass, e.g. cheap picture-frame glass

Craft soldering iron and jam jar (optional)

Craft glue, for example Tacky Glue

Iron

Seam sealant (or PVA glue)

Ruler

Baking parchment and kitchen paper

Head

1 First make the head, and needle-sculpt and paint the face following the instructions on pages 24–28. This can then be put to one side and allowed to dry, ready for use later on. Use the templates supplied on page 130 and flesh-coloured fabric.

Body

This is a contoured body made in seven sections. Four of these are print fabrics and three are part flesh and part print.

2 Cut a piece of flesh-coloured fabric 20 x 10cm (7³/₄ x 4in) and a piece of flower-printed cotton 20 x 20cm (7³/₄ x 7³/₄in). Join them together with machine stitch along the 20cm (7³/₄in) side. Press the seam down to the print fabric. Double the fabric lengthways with the seam on the outside and running horizontally.

3 Take the Centre Front template (page 130) and place it on the fold. Put the Centre Back template alongside with at least 2cm (³/₄in) between them. Align the horizontal seam line marked on the pattern pieces with the fabric seam.

4 With the pencil, mark around the Centre Front template and then the Centre Back template.

5 Take the pattern pieces for the Side Front and Side Back (see page 131), and draw around these once on to a doubled piece of flower-printed cotton.

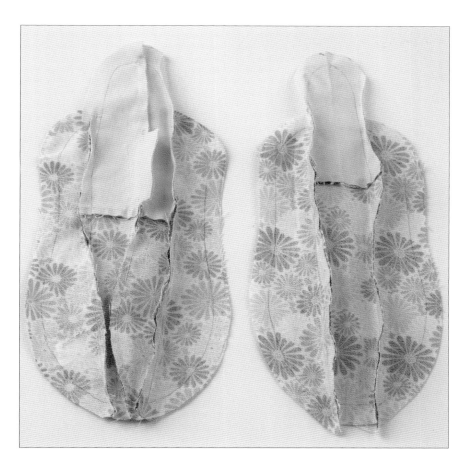

6 Machine stitch the centre-back seam on the Centre Back section, leaving the opening unstitched. Cut out the Centre Back section, leaving a 3mm (⅛in) seam allowance on the stitched centre-back seam and a 6mm (¼in) seam allowance on the unstitched side seam. Cut out the Centre Front section with a 6mm (¼in) seam allowance.

7 Cut out the Side Front and Side Back pieces with a 6mm (¼in) seam allowance all round.

8 Pin a Side Front section to the Centre Front section right sides facing, matching the bottom of the Side Front section with the bottom of the Centre Front section. The top of the Side Front section should be aligned with the neck mark on the Centre Front section. Pin the other Side Front section to the Centre Front section in the same way. Also pin the Side Back sections to the Centre Back.

9 Stitch the seams and trim the seam allowance to 3mm (⅛in).

10 Open out the body front and body back pieces and pin them together, right sides facing, all around the side seams. Machine stitch the seams, leaving the gap at the back for stuffing, and trim the seam allowance to 3mm (⅛in).

Front

Back

11 Using forceps, pull the body piece right side out, pushing out the neck, shoulders and hips. Fill the body through the opening (see page 19). Begin by stuffing the neck firmly as it must support the head. Next fill the shoulders and the hips, again firmly as they must support the jointing of the arms and legs. Fill the rest of the body, pushing the stuffing around with the forceps to create a curvy body shape. Ladder stitch the back closed (see pages 42–43).

Legs and feet

12 First, make the fairy feet following the instructions on pages 36–37. Use the template provided on page 130. For the legs, take a piece of striped cotton fabric 30 x 30cm (11¾ x 11¾in). Double it with right sides together and place the Leg pattern (from page 131) on to the fabric. Draw around it twice to make two legs. Make sure that the ankle of the leg is slightly wider than the ankle of the fairy foot. Machine stitch around both legs, leaving the ankle open. Cut out with a 3mm (⅛in) seam allowance on the stitched seams and a 6mm (¼in) seam allowance at the ankle.

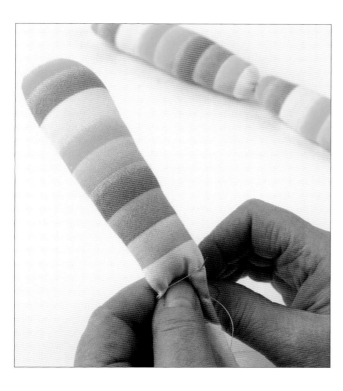

13 Pull both legs the right way out with forceps. Stuff each leg from the top downwards until the filling is 1cm (½in) above the knee joint. To make the knee joint, take a long darner and a length of thread that matches the fabric. Attach the thread at the back of the knee then bring it tightly around the knee and catch the fabric with a small stitch at the front. Repeat this twice and fasten off firmly.

14 Stuff the rest of the leg to the ankle.

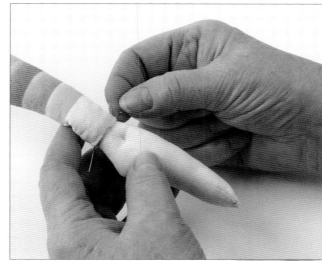

15 Push a fairy foot into the ankle at the bottom of one of the legs and ensure there is enough stuffing to keep the ankle firm. Pin the foot in place and stitch around it securely.

16 Complete both legs in the same way.

Arms and hands

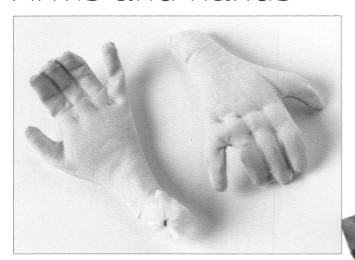

17 Make a pair of simple hands, as described on pages 32–33, using the template provided on page 131.

18 Take a piece of cotton batik fabric 24 x 18cm (9½ x 7in). Double it with right sides together. Place the Arm pattern piece (see page 131) on the fabric and draw around it. Do this twice to make two arms. As with the legs, make sure the wrist is slightly wider than the wrist on the hand. Machine stitch around the arms, leaving the wrist open.

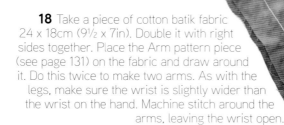

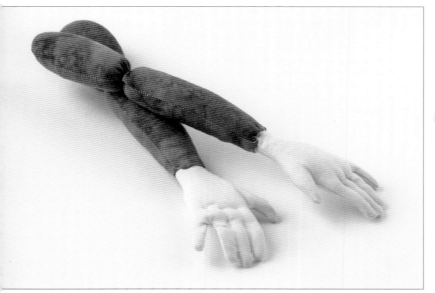

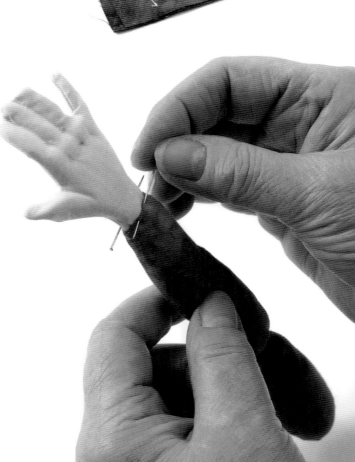

19 Cut out both arms with a 3mm (⅛in) seam allowance on the stitched seams and a 6mm (¼in) seam allowance at the wrists. Complete both arms in exactly the same way as the legs, jointing them at the elbow. Insert the hands and attach them as you did the feet.

Joining the arms and legs to the body

20 Take a long doll needle and a good length of extra-strong thread. Attach the thread to the hip on the left side of the body, on the seam. Hold the left leg next to the body and pull the needle through from the inside to the outside of the leg. Thread on a button and take the needle back again, through the button, through the leg and through the body at the hip to come out in the corresponding place on the other side.

21 Hold the right leg in place and push the needle through the top of the leg, as you did on the other side. Thread on a button, then take the needle back again through the button, leg and body, and out through the button on the other side. Repeat this once more, pulling the thread tightly as you do so. Finish off securely.

22 Attach the arms to the shoulders in the same way.

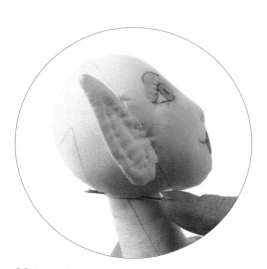

23 Make the ears and attach them to the head, as explained on page 29. Attach the head to the body (see page 29).

Costuming

Now we come to the really fun part. First, we will make the skirt for the doll. This is made from synthetic organza, which is heated with a craft heat gun. The method for doing this is shown on page 13.

24 Cut about eight triangles from the synthetic organza. I have used two colours, and the triangles are approximately 25cm (9¾in) across the base and 40cm (15¾in) down to the point. Distress the surface of each triangle using a heat gun, then pin them on to the waist of the doll.

25 Make twenty to thirty layered organza flowers following the instructions below.

Organza flowers

These are fun and simple to make using polyester organza, which you can heat-treat to give added texture. Use the templates on page 132 to cut a variety of organza petal shapes, then layer them and secure them with a few beads in the centre. A soldering iron with a tip suitable for use on textiles makes quick work of cutting out and seals the edges as it cuts. The finished flowers could be embellished around the petal edges using craft glue and gilding flakes.

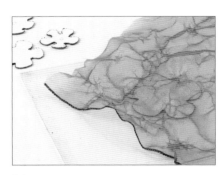

26 Place your template under a sheet of glass and lay the heat-treated organza over the top. Glass from a cheap picture frame works well.

27 Plug in the soldering iron, keeping it in a jam jar when not in use. Allow it to heat up.

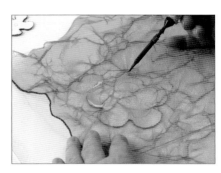

28 Hold the organza in place with one hand and carefully draw around the template with the tip of the soldering iron.

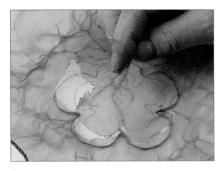

29 Carefully remove the cut-out shape.

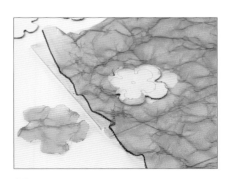

30 Cut out as many shapes as you need – four or five per flower.

31 Place four or five cut flower shapes together, pinch at the centre and stitch them together with a bead or two.

32 Pin then stitch the flowers on to the doll around the top of the skirt and also at the ankles, knees, wrists, elbows and neck.

Hair

This is always the last piece of the doll to be added. For this doll, I have used a piece of bleached Tibetan lamb skin, which is fine, wispy and incredibly soft. I have coloured it with fabric dye.

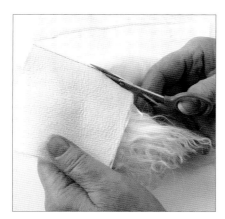

33 On the back of the lamb skin draw a square 10 x 10cm (4 x 4in). Cut it out with very small, sharp scissors, making sure you do not trap any of the fleece in the scissors. To do this, push the scissors along the skin at the base of the fleece.

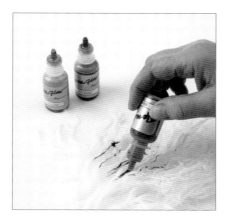

34 Apply the fabric dye to the fleece direct from the bottle. Stroke it on in the direction of the fleece. I have used three different coloured dyes – violet, turquoise and red.

35 When you have applied several streaks of dye in various colours, rub the colours into the hair and blend them together using a handful of kitchen paper. Make sure most of the hair is coloured.

63

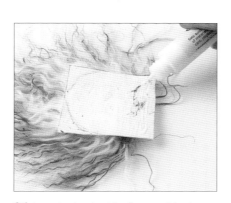

36 Lay the lamb skin fleece-side down, with the fleece all lying in one direction. Mark a curve on one side where the back of the head will join the neck. On the opposite side, apply a line of craft glue and fold over the cut edge. This will be attached to the doll's forehead.

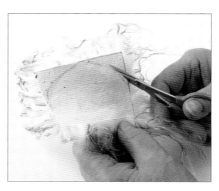

37 Cut around the marked curve and check that the hair fits around the doll's ears. Trim it down to fit if necessary.

38 Run a line of craft glue along the top of the forehead and around the back. Also put a little glue on the skin-side of the fleece. Leave it for a few minutes and then position the hair on the doll's head. Hold it in place for a few minutes until it has stuck fast. You can now comb the doll's hair gently and arrange it how you wish. Hairspray can be used to hold it in place.

Wings

A template for the wings is provided on page 132. Make two copies of it and join them in the centre to make a single shape. The wings are made by layering heat-treated organza and Angelina fibres, then adding surface stitching, beads and wired designer cord in order to sculpt the wings into shape. Variations on this basic theme are easy to achieve by simply altering the shape of the template, and varying the colours, materials and embellishments used.

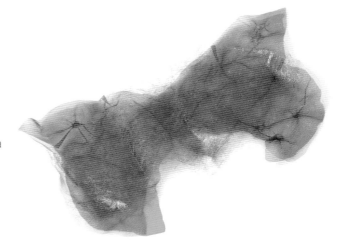

39 Heat two pieces of synthetic organza – one pink and one turquoise – with a craft heat gun to give a puckered surface (see page 13). Be careful not to over-heat the organza or burn holes that are too big. Place the two pieces of organza one on top of the other.

40 Create a thin sheet of fused Angelina fibres large enough to cover the wing area following the instructions on page 13. Lay it on top of the organza. This will give the wings a beautiful, iridescent quality.

41 Lay the organza and Angelina layers on top of the template (you will be able to see the pattern outline through the layers). Use scissors to cut out the wings, making them slightly bigger than the template.

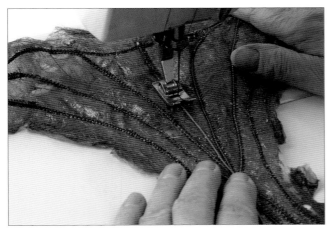

42 Create the veins using the wired designer cord. Cut two lengths of wire 50cm (19¾in) long and two 40cm (15½in) long. Lay the two longer lengths across the wings to make the upper and lower veins, and the two shorter lengths down the sides. Pin the wires in place and leave 8cm (3¼in) protruding at both ends – these will be finished off later.

43 Choose a thread colour that works well with the wings then, using a wide satin stitch and short stitch length, machine stitch along the lower and upper wires. Next, satin stitch the end wires in place. Your wings should now be strong enough to hold their shape.

44 Cut five more wires and lay them across the wings. The ends of these wires should touch the stitched wires on either side. Satin stitch them on to the wings.

45 Bend the 8cm (3¼in) lengths of wire at the corners of the wings into circles and thread on some beads. Secure them with satin stitch to form loops at the tips of the wings, as shown above.

46 Melt the edges of the wings using a heat gun to give them a ragged finish.

47 Pin the wings to the fairy's back and stitch them in place to complete your doll.

Moon Flower

The methods and materials used for my midnight fairy are very similar to those used for Peaseblossom, the flower fairy. I have chosen cotton fabrics in dark blues with silver accents, and organza in midnight blue and purple. Moon Flower's hair is bleached Tibetan lamb skin and the wings are white organza and silver and white Angelina.

Anastasia

The woodland nymph is a whimsical figure sitting in a reverie, contemplating the butterfly on her hand. She is a fixed-pose doll using many materials, some of which can be retrieved from used clothing. She has a four-part head which is needle-sculpted with drawn features. She has individual wired-finger hands, and feet with stab-stitched toes.

Head and face

1 Make the head and the needle-sculpted face following the instructions on pages 24–28. Put to one side.

YOU WILL NEED

Templates (pages 133–134)

Flesh-coloured cotton fabric: 25cm (¼yd)

Batik cotton fabric: 50cm (½yd)

Strip of cotton scrim: 20.5 x 46cm (8 x 18in)

Old knitted garment with brown ribbing for hair

Old piece of knitwear or felt for leaves

Gold seed beads

Three 30cm (12in), 6mm (¼in) chenille sticks (pipe cleaners)

Sewing machine with open-toe quilting foot, darning foot and new needle

250g (½lb) bag of good polyester stuffing

25.5cm (10in) embroidery hoop

Extra-strong upholstery thread for jointing

Quilting thread for needle-sculpting and closing seams after stuffing

Basic sewing kit of sewing needle, scissors, pins, 12cm (5in) forceps or hemostats and polyester threads in a variety of colours to match the fabrics used

Long doll needles for jointing

Long, fine darning needle, size 7, or beading needle

Chopstick or stuffing tool

Finger-turning tools

Sharp pencil or mechanical pencil

Vanishing fine-line pen

Seam sealant (or PVA glue)

Face-colouring equipment (see pages 16–17)

Textile paints

Baking parchment

Pink hot-fix Angelina fibres for butterfly

Fine beading wire

Ears

2 Take a piece of flesh-coloured fabric, fold it double and draw around two ear shapes using the template provided on page 134. Use a sharp pencil to ensure a fine line. Machine stitch around the outlines, leaving the opening. Use flesh-coloured thread and very small stitches.

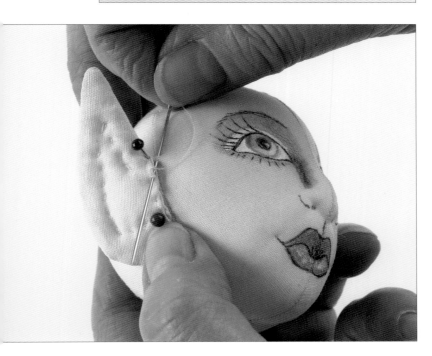

3 Cut out the ears with a 3mm (⅛in) seam allowance. Make the allowance for the opening 6mm (¼in) as it needs to be turned in after stuffing. Turn the ears out the right way and stuff them fairly lightly.

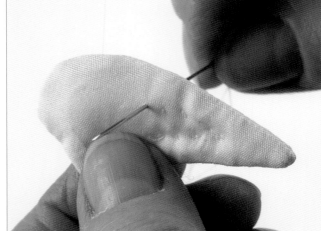

4 Using the vanishing fine-line pen, mark on the inner ear by drawing a faint outline approximately 6mm (¼in) inside each ear. Stab stitch along the line using flesh-coloured thread, leaving a gap level with the opening.

5 For each ear, turn the seam allowance into the opening and stitch it closed. Pin an ear on to each side of the head, laying the stitched opening along the side seam and aligning the top of the opening with the eyes. Stitch the ears in place.

Body

When using batik cotton fabric the colours will vary a lot. You can choose which sections to use for the different body parts before cutting them out. Allow for the body being cut from double fabric and the limbs from a single layer of fabric. Make sure you plan this out so that you have enough fabric.

6 Fold the piece of batik cotton in half on the grain, right sides together. Lay the three template pieces for the body on the fabric with the Lower Front Body on the fold and the grain marks going with the selvedge (see page 133). Trace around the templates with an ordinary pencil or a white pencil (the white pencil will show up better on a dark fabric). Also mark in the darts.

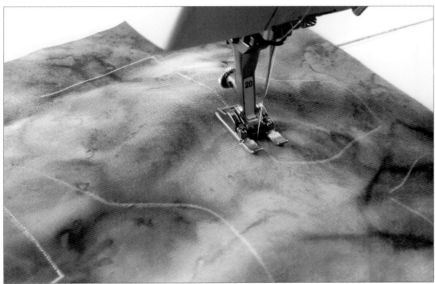

7 Machine stitch along the centre-back seam of the Body Back, leaving the opening, and the centre-front seam of the Upper Body Front.

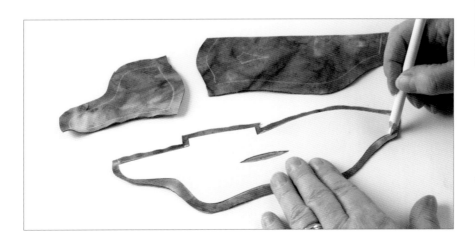

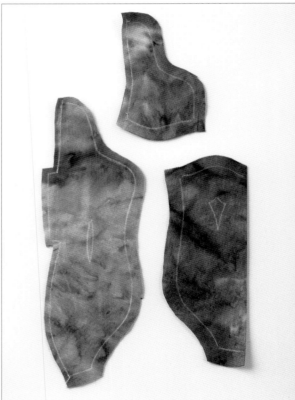

8 Cut out the three body pieces. Leave a 3mm (⅛in) seam allowance on the machined seams and 6mm (¼in) on the other sides that are still to be machined. Do not cut out the darts.

9 Turn the body pieces over and place the paper templates on top. Mark in the darts and the seams on the reverse of each piece of fabric.

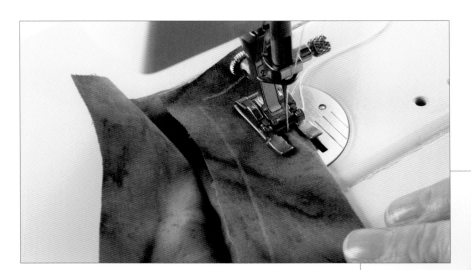

10 Stitch in the darts – two on the Body Back and two on the Lower Body Front.

11 Open out the two Body Front pieces and pin them together, right sides facing, matching the marked sewing lines. Stitch the seam, then trim to 3mm (⅛in).

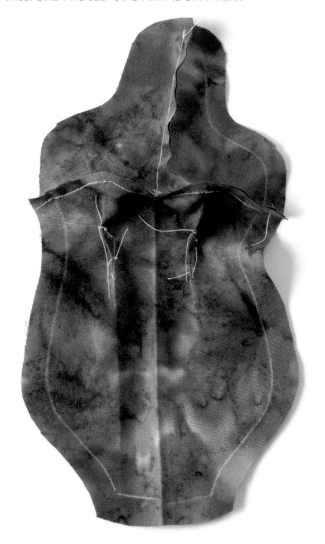

12 Open out the Body Back and pin it to the Body Front, right sides facing, matching the sewing lines. Stitch all around the side seams and trim them to 3mm (⅛in). Use forceps to pull the body right-side out and push around the seams inside to flatten them. Stuff firmly, making sure the neck, the shoulders and the hips are extra firm for holding the head and the limbs (see page 19). Close the back opening with ladder stitch (see pages 42–43).

Arms and hands

The fabric for the arms is first embroidered using free-machine embroidery. Transfer the templates from page 134 and free-machine embroider all four pieces before cutting them out. This will be more economical with fabric.

13 On a single layer of fabric draw around one arm template piece, then turn it over and draw round it again. Stretch the fabric into a 25.5cm (10in) embroidery hoop with the drawn arm shapes in the centre. If you wish, draw your chosen design on to each shape using a vanishing fine-line pen. Thread the sewing machine with your chosen thread and adjust it for free-machine embroidery (see box right). Fill each arm shape with the stitched design, overlapping the marked outlines. I have used a simple leaf design.

Free-machine embroidery

To prepare your sewing machine, lower the feed dogs, remove the presser foot and replace it with a darning foot. There is now no feed to pull the fabric through the machine and you can move the fabric freely underneath the needle. The presser foot lever should be lowered to engage the top tension. The fabric will need to be placed in a hoop to keep it taut while machining, remembering to place it so the back of the fabric lies flat against the machine bed. Now stitch away as you wish. You may find it useful to use a vanishing fine-line pen to draw in the pattern you wish to follow before you start.

14 Repeat step 13 for the other arm. You should now have four embroidered pieces – two for each arm. Cut out all four pieces with a 1cm (½in) seam allowance.

Tip

Make the embroidered design as simple or as complex as you wish. Here I have used a single layer of stitching in one colour to show you how effective a simple design can be. For Anastasia, however, I overlaid three layers of stitching in shades of pink, purple and red.

15 Pin both sides of each arm together with the embroidered sides facing and machine stitch them together along the sewing lines. Leave them open at the wrist. Turn both arms right-side out. Stuff them firmly to about 1cm (½in) from the wrist.

Tip

Make sure the wrists of the hands are narrower than the wrists of the arms so that they slot in comfortably.

16 Make a left and a right hand with individual fingers following the instructions on pages 34–35. Turn in the seam at the wrist of the arm. Push a hand into the end of each arm. Make sure the hands are the right way up and orientated correctly.

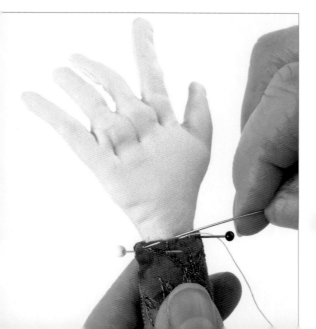

17 Pin then stitch each hand in place using ladder stitch (see pages 42–43).

Legs and feet

These are made more or less identically to the arms and hands.

18 Draw out the leg template (see page 134) on a single layer of fabric four times to make a pair of legs, put the fabric in an embroidery hoop and free-machine embroider over each leg shape as described on page 73. I have embroidered the legs using green and blue thread – one side of each leg in a different colour from the other. The legs were then constructed and stuffed exactly like the arms. The feet were made following the method shown on pages 36–37 and attached to the legs in the same way as the hands were attached to the arms. Make sure the feet are angled correctly – they should point downwards – and that you have a left and a right leg.

Joining the limbs to the body

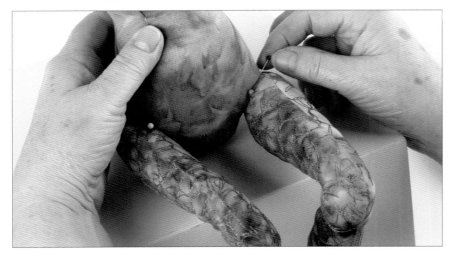

19 Place the doll on a box or a shelf and pin the legs to the body, just below the hips, so that the doll is in a good sitting position. Make sure you pin the legs on the correct sides of the body.

Attaching feet and hands

Always make sure you have a left and a right hand or foot before attaching them to the limbs. Take time to position them so that they look right, then pin them in place before stitching securely. Sew a piece of ribbon or trim around the wrist or ankle to cover the seam if you wish, or add a row of beads.

Hands: push the chenille sticks protruding from the wrist into the arm. Tuck the cotton edge inside the arm and turn under the fabric of the arm at the wrist. Pin then ladder stitch the hand in place.

Feet: feet are not strengthened with chenille sticks, so it is important to achieve a firm ankle. Make sure you have enough stuffing in both the foot and the leg before you join them together. Push all the fabric edges in and join with ladder stitch.

20 When you are satisfied with the position of the legs, stitch them securely in place using ladder stitch.

21 With the doll still seated, position the arms and pin them to the body so that the tops of the arms are level with the shoulders. Ladder stitch them in place.

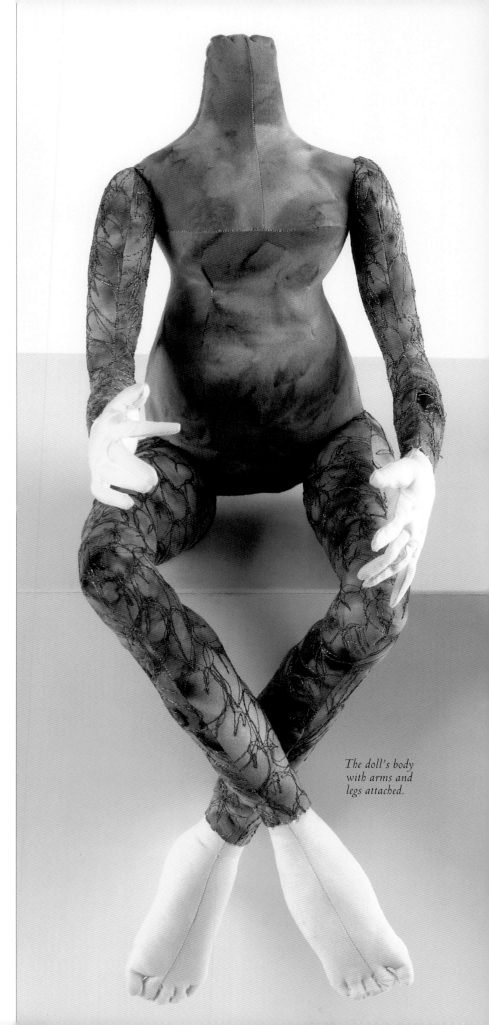

The doll's body with arms and legs attached.

Costume

Anastasia's clothes are very simple to make, but effective. Begin by taking a piece of scrim and colouring it with textile paints to coordinate with the batik fabric. Tear or cut off some strips to decorate the wrists, ankles, shoulders and hips. The more ragged they are the better.

22 Tear an uneven length of the dyed scrim for the hips. Pin it in folds and gathers around the hips and stitch it in place.

23 Pin another strip unevenly around the shoulders so that it drapes down in a v-shape at the front. Stitch it in place.

24 Tie thin strips of scrim around the ankles.

25 Decorate the wrists in the same way.

Making leaves to decorate the body

I have used old sweaters for the leaves and for the hair. You could use any old piece of clothing with a suitable colour and texture. Felt can also be used.

26 Put some green or neutral knitwear into a circular embroidery frame. Free-machine stitch approximately thirty different leaf shapes in a variety of designs and using different coloured backgrounds. Set up the machine for free embroidery as described on page 73. Make each leaf 1–1.5cm (½in) long.

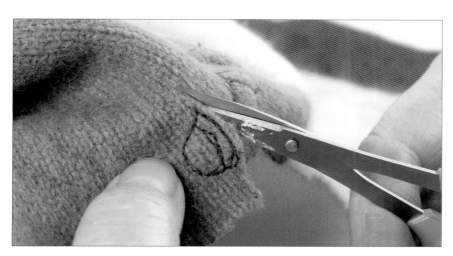

27 Cut out each leaf individually, taking care not to cut through any of the stitching lines.

28 Pin the leaves on to the doll's costume – around the hips, across the body and at the ankles and wrists. Position them so that they hang downwards and overlap them slightly.

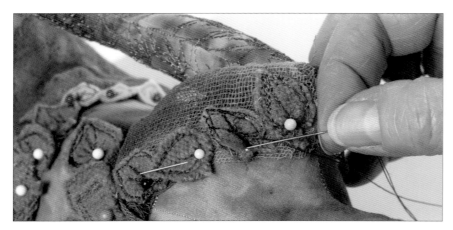

29 When you are happy with the result, stitch each leaf in place with one or two small stitches through the stem. These will be hidden by the beads that are attached later.

30 Using a fine needle or beading needle, bring the thread through the stem of one of the leaves and thread on five or six gold seed beads. Take the thread down through the fabric to form a loop and bring it up through the stem of the next leaf along. Repeat this process until as many leaves as you wish are decorated with beads.

31 To finish, decorate the shoulders with two or three loops of gold seed beads of varying lengths. Paint the finger and toe nails using a Micron Pigma pen in red.

The completed costume, front and back views.

Attaching the head

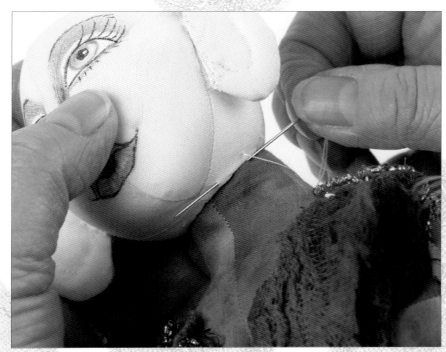

32 Push a space into the back of the head at the back opening. Push the neck into this space, or lever it in using forceps. Pin the head in place while making sure it is correctly positioned. Ladder stitch to secure the head to the neck using flesh-coloured thread.

Hair

The hair is made from three strips of ribbing cut from an old brown sweater.

33 Cut a piece of ribbing 20cm (7¾in) wide and 12cm (4¾in) long, with the ribbing running lengthways.

34 Fold the ribbing in half across the ribs and pin it around the head, with the fold level with the tips of the ears.

35 Stitch the hair in place along the fold using brown thread.

36 Snip along the lines of ribbing up to about 1cm (½in) from the fold to create strips 1cm (½in) wide around the head.

37 Cut another piece of ribbing, this time 18cm (7in) wide and 12cm (4¾in) long with the ribs running lengthways. Fold it in half as before and secure it just above the first layer of hair. Snip along the lengths of ribbing.

38 Cut the last piece of ribbing 12cm (4¾in) long and 10cm (4in) wide with the ribs running lengthways. Fold it into a piece 12 x 5cm (4¾ x 2in). Pin it on top of the head with the fold at the back and covering the top part of the other two layers of hair. This will be the fringe.

39 Stitch the hair in place across the top of the head. Snip along the ribbing as before. Using a fine needle and thread, lay a length of gold seed beads over the top of the head. Take the thread back under the hair and repeat two or three times to create a decorative gold hairband. Secure the thread under the hair.

The butterfly

Begin by preparing a solid sheet of pink Angelina (see the instructions below).

40 Draw around the template provided on page 134 using a vanishing fine-line pen and cut out the butterfly shape.

41 Bend the wings up slightly and over-sew a double length of fine beading wire along the middle of the butterfly. Separate the ends of the wire to make the antennae and curl them over at the tips using forceps. Twist the folded end of the wire together to make the body.

42 Pin and then stitch the butterfly to Anastasia's hand.

Heat-fusing Angelina fibres

Take a small clump of hot-fix Angelina fibres.

Place it between two sheets of baking parchment and press with a hot iron.

The fibres fuse into a solid mass.

Genevieve

Here is another version of
the wood nymph made from
exactly the same templates and
instructions. She has been made
from two different coloured batik
fabrics and, to keep her simple,
the free-machine embroidery has
been left out. Dyed scrim has
been used to decorate the body
and then embellished with some
buttons in complementary colours.
All the little decorative leaves and
beads have been left out to make
this doll easier to make.

Morwenna

Morwenna is a twenty-first-century steampunk doll. Her skin has a gesso and acrylic paint treatment that makes a hard surface. This is an interesting variation on the untreated fabric surface of the fairy dolls' skin. Morwenna's arms are jointed at the shoulder and she has fixed legs. Her feet and legs are single units; her boots help her to stand. She has synthetic hair and she is dressed in purples, black lace and fish-nets. A few silver chains, charms and beads have been added to finish.

YOU WILL NEED

Templates (see pages 130 and 135–137)
50cm (½yd) of white cotton fabric for the head, body, hands and legs
40 x 18cm (15¾ x 7in) of black cotton fabric for the body
50cm (½yd) of purple fabric for the arms and skirt
50cm (½yd) of black lace for the dress
250g (8oz) of polyester stuffing
One pair of black fish-net tights
One length of curly, black synthetic hair approximately 60cm (24in) long
Two 14mm (½in) silver buttons for jointing
Small silver beads for decoration
Silver-coloured charms and chain (optional)
30 x 30cm (12 x 12in) of black felt for boots
10 x 10cm (4 x 4in) of fibre board for soles
5 x 25.5cm (2 x 10in) of soft, black leather for bodice
Three 30cm (12in), 6mm (¼in) chenille sticks (pipe cleaners)
Extra-strong thread in black or purple for jointing
Quilting thread in white for sculpting

Basic sewing kit of sewing needle, scissors, pins and polyester threads in a variety of colours to match the fabrics used
Long no. 7 darning needle and long doll needle
Masking tape
Gesso
White acrylic paint
Black Pigma brush pen
Fine-line Pigma Micron pen size 01 in black
Black watercolour paint
White Fabricolour pen
Small paintbrush and 13mm (½in) flat brush
Vanishing fine-line pen
Finger-turning tools
Mechanical or fine HB pencil
White watercolour pencil
12cm (5in) forceps or hemostats
Stuffing tools or chopstick
Craft glue, for example Tacky Glue
Fine sandpaper
Iron
Paper spike
Craft knife/scalpel and cutting mat

Body

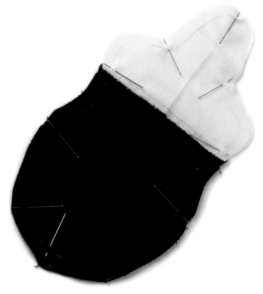

1 Cut a piece of white cotton fabric 40 x 15cm (15¾ x 6in) and machine stitch it to the piece of black cotton fabric along the 40cm (15¾in) edge. Press the seam to the black section. Fold the fabric in half with right sides together, matching the seams.

2 Place the two pattern templates for the body on to the fabric with the Body Front on the fold and the Body Back alongside (see page 137). Place the marked horizontal seam line on the stitched seam.

3 Trace around the pattern pieces carefully using a pencil on the white fabric and a white watercolour pencil on the black fabric.

4 Machine stitch along the centre-back seam of the Body Back leaving the opening. Cut out the Body Back with a 3mm (⅛in) seam allowance on the stitched seam and a 6mm (¼in) seam allowance on the unstitched seams. Cut out the Body Front with a 6mm (¼in) seam allowance.

5 Open out both body pieces and pin them together, right sides facing, aligning the centre seam and the marked stitch lines.

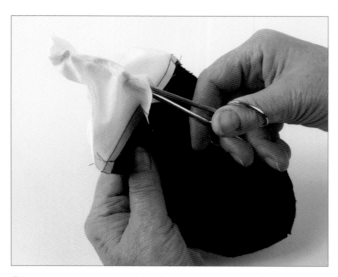

6 Machine stitch around the body on the marked stitch lines. Trim the seams to 3mm (⅛in). Pull the body through with forceps and push out all the corners and the neck.

7 Stuff the body firmly, especially the neck, shoulders and hips, and close the back with ladder stitch (see pages 42–43).

Arms and hands

8 Take a piece of purple fabric 40 x 16cm (16 x 6¼in). Fold it in half to make a piece 20 x 16cm (8 x 6¼in). Place the Arm pattern (see page 136) on top and draw around it twice using a white watercolour pencil to make two arms.

9 Machine stitch around the seams, leaving the wrists open. Cut out both arms with a 3mm (⅛in) seam allowance on the stitched seams and a 6mm (¼in) seam allowance on the wrists. Pull both arms right side out using forceps and stuff them firmly.

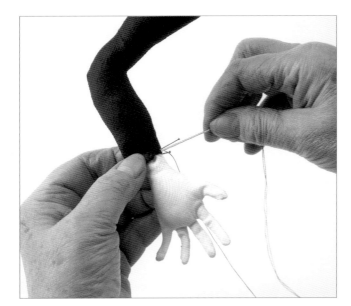

10 Make a pair of five-fingered hands using white cotton fabric. Follow the instructions on pages 34–35.

11 Push the hands into the wrists and pin then stitch them in place securely. Make sure the wrists are fully stuffed. You may need to push a little more filling in before stitching.

Making the head and painting the head, body and hands

12 Using white cotton fabric, make a fully sculpted, four-part head as described on pages 24–26 using the templates provided on page 130.

To give the doll a pale skin tone, the fabric is painted with one coat of gesso and two coats of white acrylic paint. Allow each coat to dry and sand it before applying the next. The head, hands and top of the body can be made and painted at the same time. Wrap masking tape around the wrists and bodice to protect the sleeve and body fabric.

13 Secure the head on a paper spike and paint it with a coat of gesso. Use a large brush and work it into the fabric, making it as smooth and even as possible and getting it into all the crevices.

14 Paint the hands and the top of the body at the same time. Leave everything to dry for at least an hour. Wash your brush quickly and carefully after painting.

15 When thoroughly dry, sand the painted surfaces with a fine sandpaper and blow or wipe away the dust.

16 Now paint the head, hands and body with white acrylic paint, working the paint into the surface to make it as smooth as possible. Leave everything to dry for at least an hour and sand as before.

17 Apply the second and final coat of paint to each part as in step 16. Leave to dry and sand again for a smooth, even surface.

All the painted pieces will now have a smooth and hardened surface, so take care not to crack them when handling. If you have not tried this technique before, practise on a spare head first and don't rush it.

Legs and feet

These can be made while you are waiting for the painted parts to dry. Note that you need to join the templates for the Upper Leg and Lower Leg before cutting out, see pages 136–137.

18 Take a piece of white cotton fabric 40 x 40cm (15¾ x 15¾in) and fold it in half. Place the two Leg templates on the fabric and draw around them twice to make two legs. Machine stitch around each leg, leaving the toe end and the opening at the back of the thigh open.

19 Cut out each leg with a 3mm (⅛in) seam allowance on the stitched seams and a 6mm (¼in) seam allowance across the toes and at the opening.

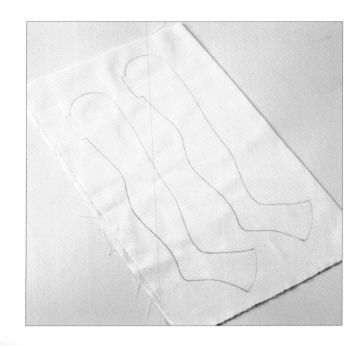

20 Re-fold each foot so that the seams are matching, pin the fabric in place and draw a curved line for the toes. Machine stitch around this line and trim the fabric, leaving a 3mm (⅛in) seam allowance.

21 Pull each leg through, pushing out the foot, and stuff firmly. Make sure each foot is set at right angles to the leg so that the doll can stand up. Close the opening at the top of the leg with ladder stitch (see pages 42–43).

Drawing and colouring the face

22 Take the Eye template (page 137) and place it in the eye socket between the two stitches marking the inner and outer eye. Hold it in place with your fingernail and draw around it very lightly with a vanishing fine-line pen. Turn the template over and repeat for the other eye.

23 Take the Mouth template (page 137) and hold it in position for the mouth. This is the centre line of the mouth. Draw a light line using a vanishing fine-line pen.

24 When you are happy with the positions of the eyes and mouth, draw over the outlines carefully with a Pigma Micron pen size 01 in black.

25 With the same pen, draw in the pupils and irises. Put in two dots for nostrils and draw in the upper lip and the middle section of the lower lip.

26 With the Pigma brush pen in black, strengthen the features and fill in the irises and the upper lip. Add short, thin eyebrows to give the face a sorrowful expression.

27 Using watercolour paint and a small brush, mix up a watery shade of black. Use this to shade the eye sockets and the lower lip. This needs to be done in a single brush stroke or it will become mixed in with the white acrylic paint underneath. Colour the eye whites and the pupils using a white Fabricolour pen.

Finishing the arms and legs

28 Cut one leg off a pair of fish-net tights and work two rows of machine stitching up the middle of it. Cut between the stitching to create two narrow fish-net stockings for your doll. Zigzag stitch along each stitched seam to strengthen it.

29 Stitch across one end of each stocking at an angle to make the foot and pull each stocking on to one leg of the doll. Trim off the top of each stocking, fold it over on to the inside of the leg and hand-stitch it in place.

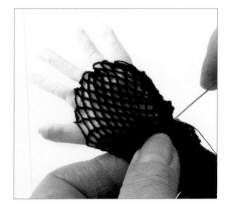

30 Cut a small piece of fish-net and fit it over one of the hands, poking the fingers through the holes. Trim off the excess fabric and hand-stitch the mitten in place. Repeat for the other hand.

Joining the arms and legs to the body

The legs need to be stitched to the body while keeping them straight and the feet flat on the ground, otherwise the doll will not be able to stand.

31 Pin the first leg to the side of the body at the hip. Hand-stitch all the way around the top of the leg two or three times to secure it using extra-strong thread. Position and attach the second leg in the same way, making sure it is level with the first leg.

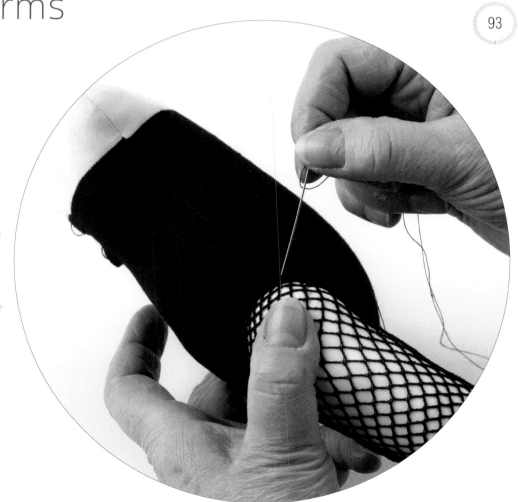

32 Attach the arms using button joints. Take a long doll needle and a good length of extra-strong thread. Attach the thread to the shoulder on the left side of the body, on the seam. Hold the left arm next to the body and pull the needle through from the inside of the arm to the outside. Thread on a small silver button and take the needle back through the button, through the arm and through the body to come out in the corresponding position on the other side.

33 Hold the right arm in place and push the needle through the top of the arm, as you did on the other side. Thread on a matching button, then take the needle back again through the button, arm and body. Repeat this once more, pulling the thread tightly as you do so. Finish off securely.

34 For the wrist cuffs, cut two pieces of soft, black leather each 1.5 x 6cm (½ x 2¼in). Wrap each one around the doll's wrists and secure with a small silver bead stitched all the way through the arm.

Costuming

35 Cut a piece of purple fabric 35 x 65cm (13¾ x 25½in), using the selvedge for one of the long sides. This will form the hem of the dress and reduce bulk.

36 Machine stitch the two short sides of the fabric together to make a tube.

37 Work a line of small running stitches 6mm (¼in) from the frayed edge at the opposite end to the hem.

38 Place the dress on the doll and pull the gathering stitches to fit. Fasten off and hand-stitch the top of the dress to the body.

39 Cut a piece of black lace 40 x 100cm (15¾ x 39½in). With the short sides going from top to bottom, pin the lace in gathers around the doll's body to reach from the top of the neck to the lower calf. Overlap the lace at the back of the doll and tuck the lace under her arms.

40 For the bodice, cut a piece of soft, black leather 22 x 4cm (8¾ x 1½in). Wrap it tightly around the doll's waist so that it holds the lace in position. Overlap it at the back and pin it in place.

41 Attach three small, silver beads to the front and to the back of the bodice. Start by attaching the thread at the front, then thread on a bead and take the thread back through the bead and right through the body to the other side. Thread on another bead and repeat in the opposite direction. Do this two or three times for each pair of beads.

42 Trim the lace around the neck if necessary, then join the lace over each shoulder using a small silver bead.

43 Run a few lines of small running stitches along the length of the purple dress and pull it into random gathers.

44 Gather random sections of the lace in the same way, and attach some silver beads here and there for decoration.

Boots

These will help your doll to stand without support, as long as she is balanced correctly and placed on a flat surface in a sheltered position.

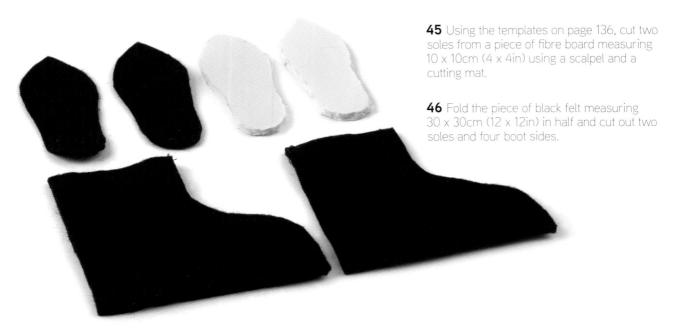

45 Using the templates on page 136, cut two soles from a piece of fibre board measuring 10 x 10cm (4 x 4in) using a scalpel and a cutting mat.

46 Fold the piece of black felt measuring 30 x 30cm (12 x 12in) in half and cut out two soles and four boot sides.

47 Join each pair of boot shapes together by machine stitching up the sides. Leave the ends open.

48 Fit each boot around one of the fibre-board soles and apply a little craft glue around the edge of the sole. Fold the edges of each boot over on to the sole and hold them in place for a few seconds.

49 When the edges of the boots are stuck down firmly, apply more glue to each sole, not too thickly, at the edges, and stick a felt sole on to the base of each boot.

Hair

50 Attach the doll's head to the body (see page 29). Unpin the opening at the back of the head and poke a hole into the stuffing with your stuffing tool or chopstick. Push the neck into the head and pin it in place. Using a small ladder stitch, attach the head to the neck by sewing all around the join.

51 I have used synthetic curly hair, which looks fantastic and is very easy to use. Hold the hair in place on the head using a few pins, then stitch it in place using the fine darning needle.

Add chains and charms to complete your steampunk-style doll.

Rhiannon

For the midnight witch, I have used the same techniques as for Morwenna, but changed to a black and red colour scheme. I put a pale green watercolour wash over the face before drawing in the features, and have used the fabric from a pair of striped socks for the mittens and a cobweb lace that I found on the internet for the dress. The witch's hat is made from black felt (templates are included on page 135) and the broom is made from a twig and a bundle of raffia. Various charms including cats, moons and stars have been added to complete the doll.

Titania

This doll is the most complex so far. I have made her with dupion silk that has been block printed with purple and gold (Jacquard Lumiere®) textile paint. If you wish to print your fabric in this way, this should be done before cutting the fabric. Instead of dupion silk, any firmly woven cotton/silk fabric can be used. She has wings made from hot-fix Angelina fibres as well as a beaded tiara and bead embroidery.

Head

1 Make a four-part needle-sculpted head with a drawn and coloured face as on pages 24–28.

Body

For the body, I have used a piece of dupion silk block printed following the method described on page 12. You can print any design you wish on to the silk or, alternatively, use a piece that already has a design printed on it. Before cutting the body pieces, you will need to join the block-printed silk to a piece of flesh-coloured cotton.

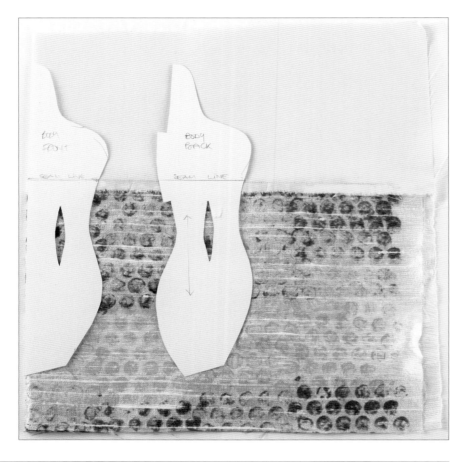

2 Cut a piece of flesh-coloured cotton 32 x 10cm (12½ x 4in) and a piece of fabric for the body 32 x 20cm (12½ x 7¾in). Seam them together along the 32cm (12½in) side and press the seam away from the flesh-coloured cotton. Fold the fabric in half with the right sides together and the seam running widthways. Place the body template pieces on the fabric with the marked seam line aligned with the seam. Place the Body Front on the fold. Draw around both pieces using a sharp pencil and mark in the darts.

3 Machine stitch along the centre-back seam on the Body Back, leaving the opening for stuffing. Cut out both pieces with a 3mm (⅛in) seam allowance on the machined seam and 6mm (¼in) on the other sides that are still to be machined. Do not cut out the darts.

4 Machine the darts on the back and front body pieces.

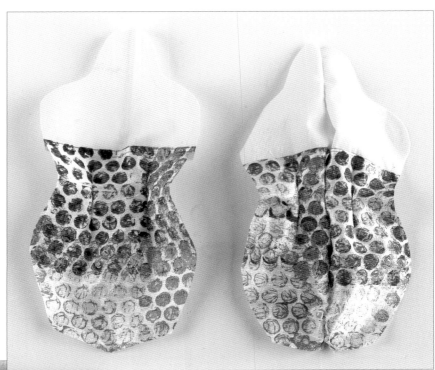

The front and back body pieces.

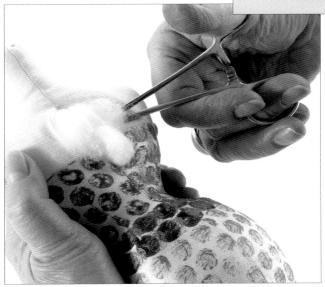

5 Pin the back and front body pieces right sides together with the bodice seams matching and machine around the side seams using small (size 1–2) stitches. Turn right-side out using the forceps and smooth out the seams with a chopstick. Stuff the body firmly, especially the neck, shoulders and hips. These parts take the strain of jointing and holding the head and need to be strong. When the body is firm enough, pin the opening together and close with ladder stitch.

Bust

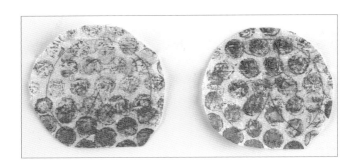

6 With a sharp pencil, draw around the pattern piece twice on a single layer of silk fabric. Cut around each shape, without cutting into the dart, with a 6mm (¼in) seam allowance. Machine in the darts.

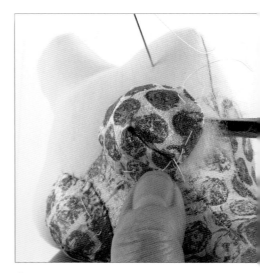

8 Stuff the bust evenly on both sides using forceps and close the opening. Remove the tacking/basting stitches.

7 Finger press the 6mm (¼in) seam to the inside of each cup and tack/baste it down. Pin each cup on to the front of the doll so that the darts match those on the body. Position the cups symmetrically and lying partly over the horizontal seam line. When you are happy with its appearance, ladder stitch the bust in place leaving a space for stuffing.

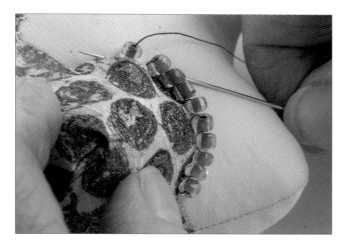

9 Sew 4mm purple beads around the top of each cup. Work in ladder stitch, threading a bead on to each stitch as you work.

The completed body.

Arms and hands

The arms are made in two pieces using a different fabric for the upper and lower arms, with a tab joint at the elbow cut from the same fabric as the upper arms. The finished hand is inserted at the wrist and ladder stitched in place.

10 On doubled fabric mark out two upper arms, two lower arms and the arm gusset. Machine stitch around the two upper arms leaving the opening. Cut them out with a 3mm (⅛in) seam allowance. For the lower arms, machine stitch the side seams down to the dashed line shown on the template. Cut out the lower arms and the two gussets with a 6mm (¼in) seam allowance. Mark the stitching line on both gussets using a sharp pencil. Pin a gusset on to the two flaps of each lower arm and machine stitch it in place. Trim the seams to 3mm (⅛in).

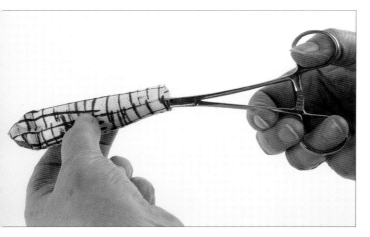

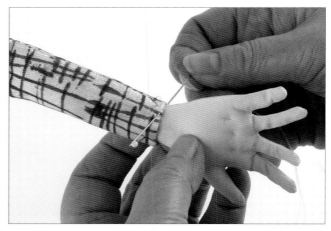

11 Turn the two lower arms in the right way and put a few stitches by hand along the bottom of each tab (marked with a dashed line on the template). This is to prevent stuffing from being pushed into the gusset tabs. Smooth the seams with a chopstick or forceps and stuff the lower arms to about 1cm (½in) above the wrist.

12 Make a right and a left five-fingered hand following the instructions on pages 34–35. Make sure the wrists of the hands are narrower than the wrists of the arms so that they slot together comfortably. Turn the seam allowance for each arm wrist into the arm, then insert the hands, pushing the chenille sticks up into the arm firmly. Make sure the hands are positioned correctly before ladder stitching them in place.

13 Turn the two upper arms in the right way, smooth the seams and stuff firmly. Close the opening with ladder stitch.

Elbow joint

14 Fit the lower arm into the upper arm within the tab joint.

15 Using extra-strong thread and a long needle, push the needle through the joint and thread on a button. Take the needle back through the button to secure it and through to the other side of the joint. Fasten a button on that side too, then take the thread through two or three times more to secure and fasten off. Pull the thread tight enough so that there is movement but the joint is held firmly.

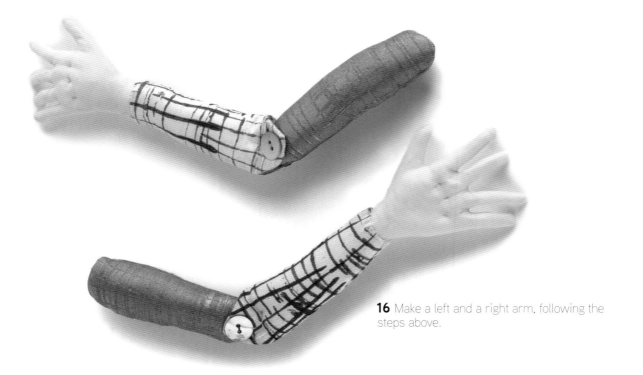

16 Make a left and a right arm, following the steps above.

Legs and feet

Like the arms, each leg is made in two pieces from two different fabrics and tab jointed together. The upper leg is cut from fabric block printed with the same design as the body but using different colours. The lower legs are shaped slightly with a calf; make sure this goes at the back when attaching the legs. The feet are made following the instructions on pages 36–37 and attached in the same way as the arms.

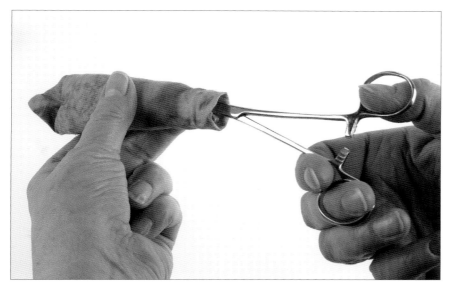

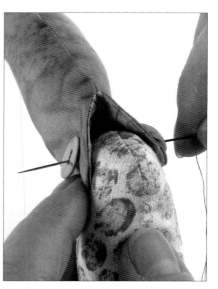

17 Make the lower legs in the same way as the lower arms. Use a contrasting fabric for the gussets. Stitch by hand across the top of the tab joint and stuff each leg firmly to about 1cm (½in) above the opening. Avoid pushing stuffing into the tab joint. Make the feet, ensuring the ankles have enough stuffing to be firm. You may need to add more stuffing before finally ladder stitching together.

18 Make the two upper legs and join them to the lower legs with a tab joint (see the instructions for making the elbow joint opposite).

Attaching the legs to the body

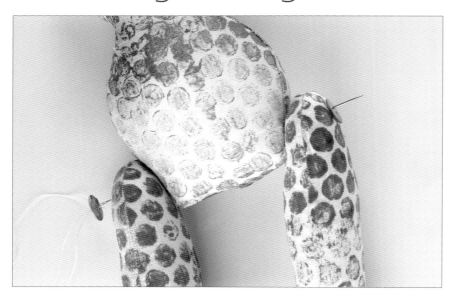

19 Use a 1m (40in) length of extra-strong thread and a 19cm (7½in) doll jointing needle. Fasten the thread securely to the side seam at the hip on one side of the doll. With a button on the outside of each leg, go through the leg, button, back through the button and leg, and through the hip to come out in exactly the same position on the other side. Repeat the process, then take the needle back through to where you started and repeat twice more. Pull the thread firmly each time you go through the body so that the legs are jointed firmly.

Attaching the arms to the body

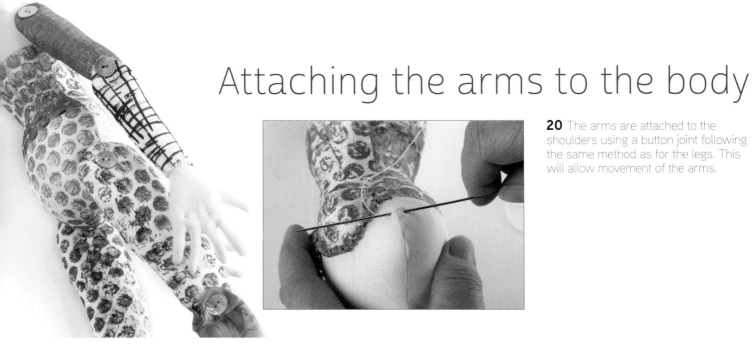

20 The arms are attached to the shoulders using a button joint following the same method as for the legs. This will allow movement of the arms.

Skirt and shoulder decorations

From cream and white tulle, cut six to eight pieces in each of the three sizes (marked A, B and C on the templates on page 140). I have singed the edges of the tulle, which gives a very pretty finish to each piece.

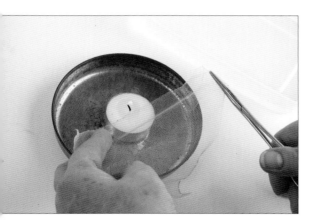

21 To singe the edges of the tulle, use a tea light placed on a saucer and have a bowl of water nearby in case of accidental flames. Light the tea light. Hold a piece of tulle with forceps at one end and by hand at the other and pull it through the bottom of the flame to create an attractive edge. Practise with a spare piece of tulle first.

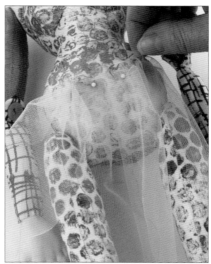

22 Pin three or four pieces of singed tulle around the hips, gathering the longest edge of each piece into random pleats and leaving the corners hanging down. Pin one or two pieces on to each shoulder, again in random folds.

23 Stitch the tulle in place at the shoulders and hips, threading on some 4mm (³/₁₆in) purple beads as you work to decorate. Put two or three beads on to the thread and pull into a circle, then stitch to the hips or shoulders where desired.

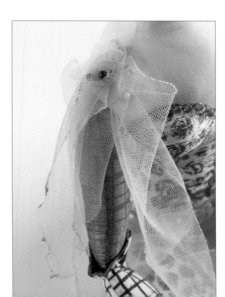

Attaching the head

See the instructions on page 29 for attaching the head to the body.

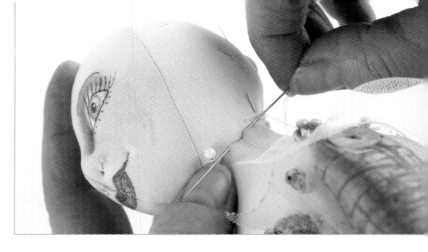

24 Remove the pins from the head opening and make a space in the stuffing. Push the head into the space and adjust it into a good position. Pin the head in place, pushing the seams of the opening inwards. Use ladder stitch to attach the head firmly and securely.

Decorating the body

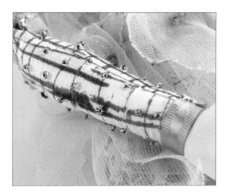

25 Stitch silver seed beads randomly over the lower arms and attach a band of gold ribbon around the wrist. Colour the finger and toe nails using a pink Micron Pigma pen.

26 Repeat on the lower legs using pink and purple seed beads. Wrap gold ribbon around the ankles and secure with stitches.

Hair

27 Cut a length of wool tops into three or four equal lengths and tease them into one mass.

28 Wind a hank of fancy yarn around a book or DVD case, cut through the hank at both ends and lay the lengths of yarn on to the wool tops in a random fashion. Cut thin strips of the fabrics used to make the doll and some strips of tulle. Lay these on to the other fibres to make the hair. Spread out the yarns and fabrics so that the bundle measures about 8cm (2in) across the middle, where the centre parting will be.

29 Machine stitch across the centre of the hank of yarns twice to hold them together securely.

30 Position the hair on the doll's head, with the machine stitching running front to back along the middle like a centre parting. Pin and then hand-stitch it in place along the line of machining.

Tiara

31 Take a 20cm (7¾in) length of fine wire and thread it with 4mm (³⁄₁₆in) purple, blue and white beads. Leave 5cm (2in) at each end bare, and bend the beaded section into three loops.

32 Attach the tiara to the top of the doll's head by embedding the ends of the wire into the hair.

Wings

The wings are made from heat-fused Angelina fibres. See page 13 for instructions on how to make these. You will need to make two lower and two upper wings. To ensure you have enough Angelina, place two template pieces (one upper and one lower wing) on to baking parchment and cover with teased-out Angelina fibres in a mix of colours. Fold over the baking parchment so the Angelina is covered on both sides and press with a hot iron until the fibres are fused together. Remove the top baking sheet. Repeat for the other two wings.

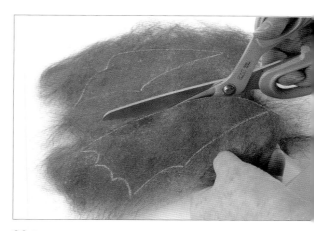

33 Place the template pieces for an upper and a lower wing in the best position on the fused Angelina. Draw around the patterns with a white pencil or vanishing fine-line pen. Cut out the pieces. Do the same again so that you have two of each type of wing.

34 Place one of the wings on to pink organza and lay it under the sewing machine. Set the machine to zigzag stitch and thread it with a purple machine embroidery thread to match the wings. Take a length of beading wire and zigzag stitch the wire in place all around the edge of each wing. Repeat for the other three wings.

35 Prepare the sewing machine for free-machine embroidery (see page 73). Trim off the excess organza around the edges of the wings and draw on the lines for the veins using a vanishing fine-line pen. Make the two left-hand wings mirror images of those on the right. Use free-machine embroidery to stitch along the veins. Now you have two pairs of wings for your fairy.

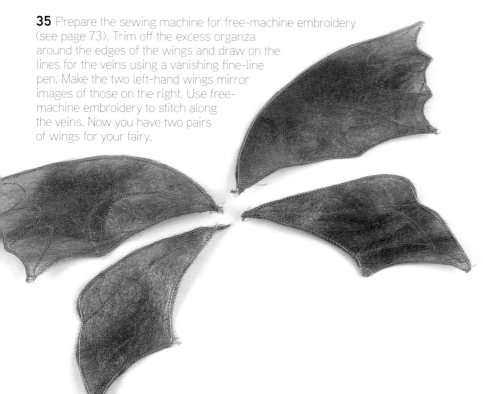

36 Arrange the wings on Titania's back and pin then stitch them in place.

Coriander

This fairy is made from the same templates and instructions. By using patterned and plain cotton fabrics acquired from a patchwork and quilting shop, no printing or dyeing was involved. The colours used are deeper and more jewel-like, giving the doll a completely different look.

Nerissa

The mermaid has webbed fingers, and a weighted tail so that she will sit independently. Her flesh parts are made using a pale cotton batik, which gives her a watery, fish-like appearance. Her face has a strange, almost alien look reminiscent of a mysterious sea creature – a look that is further enhanced by the use of abstract designs painted on to her face, arms and body using metallic paint. Her tail is a collage of appliquéd fabric triangles, shells and beads, and her hair is made from textured blue and green slub yarn that resembles dreadlocks.

YOU WILL NEED

Templates (see pages 142–143)

50cm (½yd) of pale cotton batik fabric for the body, arms, head and bag for filling

50cm (½yd) of blue cotton fabric for the tail

30 x 30cm (12 x 12in) of blue and green batik fabric for the tail fin

20 x 20cm (7¾ x 7¾in) of wadding/batting

Collection of fabric scraps in a range of blues, greens and yellows for the tail scales

30g (1½oz) of polypropylene beads for weighting the tail

250g (8oz) of polyester stuffing

Three 30cm (12in), 6mm (¼in) chenille sticks (pipe cleaners)

Quilting thread in Natural for sculpting

Assorted shells, beads and sequins for decoration

30g (1oz) of slub or fancy yarn for hair, space-dyed in shades of blue and green

30cm (12in) of craft wire for the tail fin

Basic sewing kit of sewing needle, scissors, pins and polyester threads in a variety of colours to match the fabrics used

Long no. 7 darning needle and a felting needle

Finger-turning tools

12cm (5in) forceps or hemostats

Stuffing tools or chopstick

Face-colouring equipment (see pages 16–17), including watercolour pencils in Aquamarine, Dahlia Purple, Blush Pink and Kelly Green

Lumiere® pearlescent textile paint in Turquoise

Vanishing fine-line pen

Mechanical or sharp HB pencil

White watercolour pencil

Craft glue, for example Tacky Glue

Iron

Head

Make a fully sculpted, four-part head as shown on pages 24–28 using the pale cotton batik fabric. Use the diagram right and follow the instructions below. I have made the mermaid's eyes a little longer than the fairy's and slanted them upwards at the outer corners. Her mouth is slightly wider and fuller.

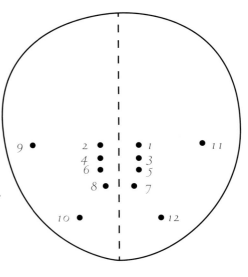

Needle-sculpting the head

1 Follow the general instructions provided on page 25 up to and including step 4.

2 At step 5, work the needle-sculpting stitches down the nose: push the needle in at 1 and out at 4; in at 4 and out at 3; in at 3 and out at 6; in at 6 and out at 5; in at 5 and out at 8 (the left nostril); in at 8 and out at 6; in at 6 and out at 7 (the right nostril).

3 Push the needle in at 7 and out at 9 (the outer corner of the left eye), then take it through at 9 and out at 12 (the right-hand corner of the mouth).

4 Push the needle in at 12 and out at 11 (the outer corner of the right eye), then take it through at 11 and out at 10 (the left-hand corner of the mouth). Push the needle in at 10 and out through the back of the head to finish off.

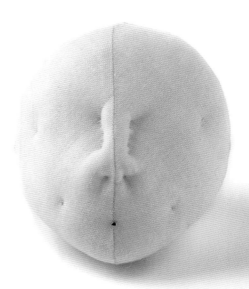

The needle-sculpted head.

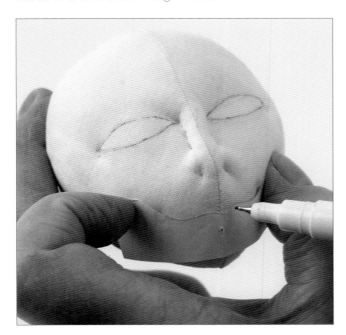

5 Use the templates provided on page 143 to draw on the eyes and the centre line of the mouth using a vanishing fine-line pen. Remember to reverse the template for the second eye.

6 Add the irises and the pupils and draw in the eyebrows and lips. When you are happy with your face, draw over the lines using a black fine-line Pigma Micron pen size 01.

7 Blacken the pupils but leave a small highlight. Use the Dahlia Purple watercolour pencil to shade around the eye socket and down the sides of the nose, leaving the eyelid white. Blend the colour with a scrap of cotton fabric. Place Aquamarine watercolour pencil under the eye and in a v-shape on the forehead. Blend the colour as before.

8 Add Blush Pink to the cheeks and blend, then fill the lips with purple, leaving highlights. Build up the colour until you are happy with the result.

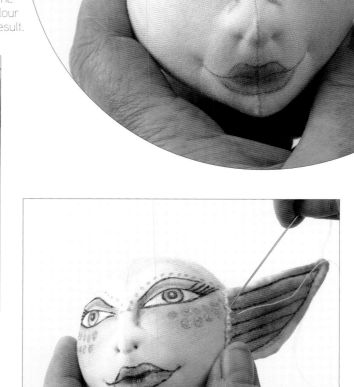

9 Colour the eyes using Kelly Green watercolour pencil and draw on the eyelashes at the corners of the eyes using the black Pigma Micron pen. Put a dot of black on each nostril and colour the eye whites with a white Fabricolour pen. Finally, decorate the face with dots of Lumiere® pearlescent textile paint in Turquoise applied straight from the bottle. If necessary, strengthen the outlines of the features using a black Pigma Micron pen size 05.

10 Use the template on page 143 to make the ears. Follow the instructions provided on page 29. After stuffing them lightly, add hand-stitching in the pattern shown above. Draw over the stitched lines using the black Pigma Micron pen size 05 and colour each ear using the purple, aquamarine and pink watercolour pencils.

11 Attach the ears to the head, aligning the top of each ear with the corner of the eye and laying it along the side seam of the head (see the photograph above).

The finished face.

Arms and webbed hands

These are made in one piece using the template on page 142.

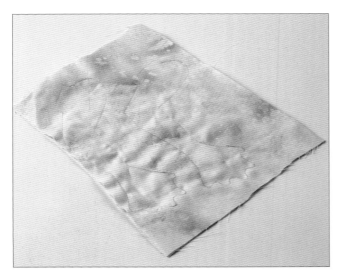

12 Trace the template twice on to doubled pale cotton batik fabric using pencil. Machine stitch around each arm on the outline, leaving the opening for stuffing.

13 Cut out each arm, leaving a 3mm (⅛in) seam allowance. Pull each arm the right way out using forceps. Make sure each fingertip is properly pulled through.

14 With your vanishing fine-line pen, draw the fingers on to each webbed hand. Either draw these freehand, or cut away the 'webbing' around the fingers on the template and use this to draw around.

15 Machine stitch along the v-shaped lines between each finger.

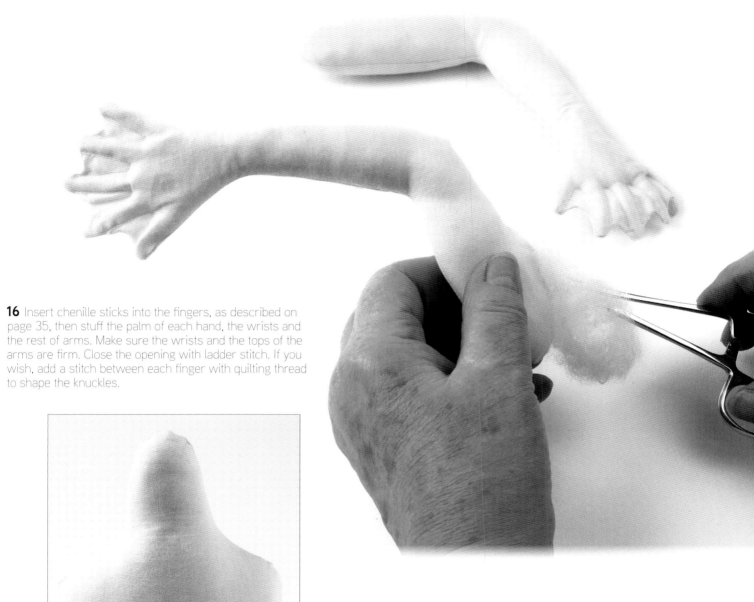

16 Insert chenille sticks into the fingers, as described on page 35, then stuff the palm of each hand, the wrists and the rest of arms. Make sure the wrists and the tops of the arms are firm. Close the opening with ladder stitch. If you wish, add a stitch between each finger with quilting thread to shape the knuckles.

Body

17 Place the template for the Body (see page 143) on a piece of doubled pale cotton batik fabric, draw around it using a pencil and machine stitch all around it on the marked line, leaving the opening at the bottom.

18 Cut out the body, leaving a 3mm (⅛in) seam allowance, and stuff firmly. Close the gap using ladder stitch.

Tail

19 Place the two pattern pieces for the tail (see page 142) on to doubled blue cotton fabric. Draw around each one using a white watercolour pencil.

20 Machine stitch the dart in the two Tail Back pieces. Machine stitch the centre-back seam of the Tail Back pieces and the centre-front seam of the Tail Front. Cut out both pieces with a 3mm (⅛in) seam allowance on the stitched seams and a 6mm (¼in) seam allowance on the unstitched seams.

21 For the appliqué you will need pieces of fabric in a range of blues, greens and yellows. I used plain cotton fabric in five different colours, some dupion silks, an embroidered chiffon fabric, some felt and some brocade. Cut each piece of fabric into a number of small triangles – do this by eye to avoid them all being the same shape and size.

22 Open out one of the tail pieces, either the front or the back. On the right side, stick a row of overlapping triangles along the base in a random colour arrangement, with the points toward the base. Extend the triangles beyond the edges of the background fabric and ensure all of the fabric is covered. Attach each triangle with a small dab of craft glue on the back – not too much or it will soak through and be visible on the front.

23 When you have stuck down one row of triangles, put a contrasting thread in your sewing machine and topstitch each piece, roughly following the shape of the triangle.

24 Continue row by row, overlapping the triangles to make a scale-type pattern. This is intended to look haphazard and irregular, with the frayed edges adding to the effect.

25 Repeat to add triangles to the second tail piece.

26 When you have covered both tail pieces with the appliqué, join the side seams and the bottom of the tail, right sides together. Trim off the excess fabric.

27 Pin a piece of doubled blue and green batik fabric to a layer of wadding/batting and draw around the template for the tail fin using a pencil or a white watercolour pencil. The template is provided on page 143.

28 Machine stitch around the outline, leaving the end open for turning. Cut out with a seam allowance of 3mm (⅛in).

29 Turn the fin right side out and push the length of craft wire into the fin to fit all around the outer edge. Hold the wire in place with pins.

30 Machine stitch around the outer edge of the fin to form a channel around the wire. Fit the fin into the bottom of the tail. Pin then hand-sew the fin firmly in place with ladder stitch.

31 Stuff the tail up to just above the bend using forceps.

32 Use a selection of beads, sequins and small shells to decorate the tail.

33 Make a small bag from the body fabric, finished size 6.5 x 9cm (2½ x 3½in). Fill it with polypropylene beads and sew it up securely. Put the bag into the tail. This will weight the mermaid and help her to sit.

Finishing the body

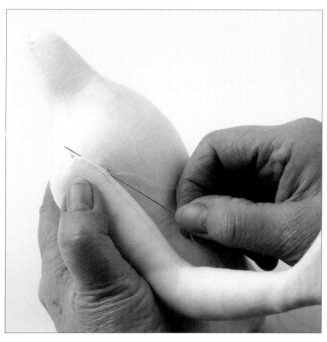

34 Attach the arms to the body using ladder stitch.

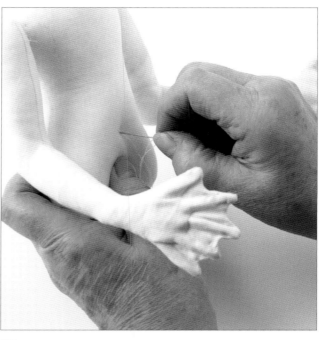

35 Make the belly button using two or three needle-sculpting stitches taken right through the doll's body and back again.

36 For the mermaid's top, use the same fabric triangles that you used for the scales on the tail. Pin them on to the mermaid's chest in the shape of a bikini top. When you have a few in place, hand-stitch them with beads and sequins to secure them. Add a few more and continue to build up the shape of the top on the front and back of the doll.

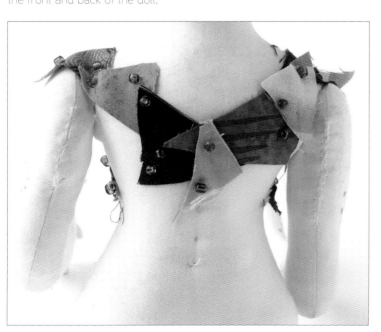

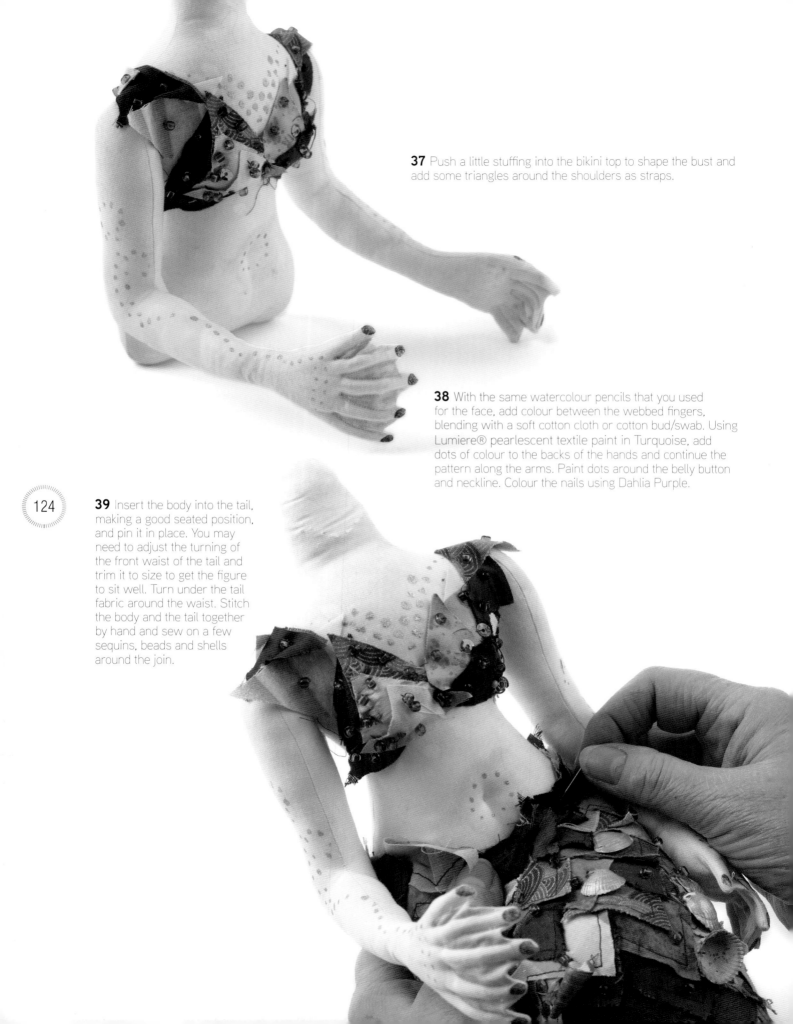

37 Push a little stuffing into the bikini top to shape the bust and add some triangles around the shoulders as straps.

38 With the same watercolour pencils that you used for the face, add colour between the webbed fingers, blending with a soft cotton cloth or cotton bud/swab. Using Lumiere® pearlescent textile paint in Turquoise, add dots of colour to the backs of the hands and continue the pattern along the arms. Paint dots around the belly button and neckline. Colour the nails using Dahlia Purple.

39 Insert the body into the tail, making a good seated position, and pin it in place. You may need to adjust the turning of the front waist of the tail and trim it to size to get the figure to sit well. Turn under the tail fabric around the waist. Stitch the body and the tail together by hand and sew on a few sequins, beads and shells around the join.

Hair

40 Cut the thick slub yarn, space-dyed in shades of blue and green, into varied lengths. Lay them in a pile, with all the lengths lying in roughly the same direction.

41 Attach the doll's head to the body (see page 29). Unpin the opening at the back of the head and poke a hole into the stuffing with your stuffing tool or chopstick. Push the neck into the head and pin it in place. Using a small ladder stitch, attach the head to the neck by sewing all around the join.

42 Place a layer of yarns over the head and needle-felt them in place with a felting needle. Add more layers until you are happy with the effect. To form a chunky, layered style, start with longer lengths for the first layers and end with shorter lengths around the top of the head.

43 To finish, sew a few beads, sequins and shells into the hair, as shown. The finished mermaid can be seen on page 115.

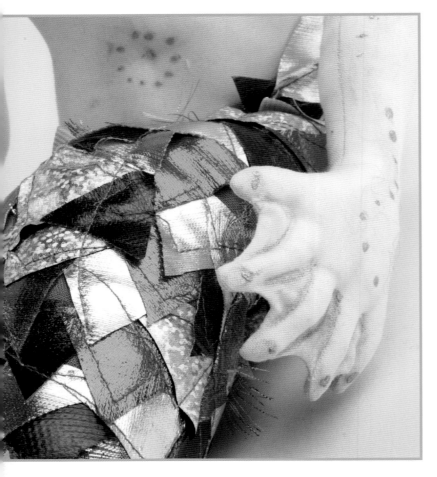

Merina

For my alternative mermaid design I have used the same batik fabric for all the skin parts, but replaced the fabric scraps with metallics for the scales and the tail fin. The body is decorated using Lumiere® pearlescent textile paint and the hair is made from a hank of sari silk, which is sold for hand knitting.

Templates

All the templates in the book are actual size. You can trace them on to copy paper or photocopy them on to card. They should then be cut out accurately so that you can trace around them on to the fabric. Card patterns can be re-used and will last a long time; they are also a little firmer to draw around. When you have cut out your templates, write on what they are straight away and mark on any additional information such as grain lines, darts and seams.

Miranda

and Bluebelle variation, pages 40–53.

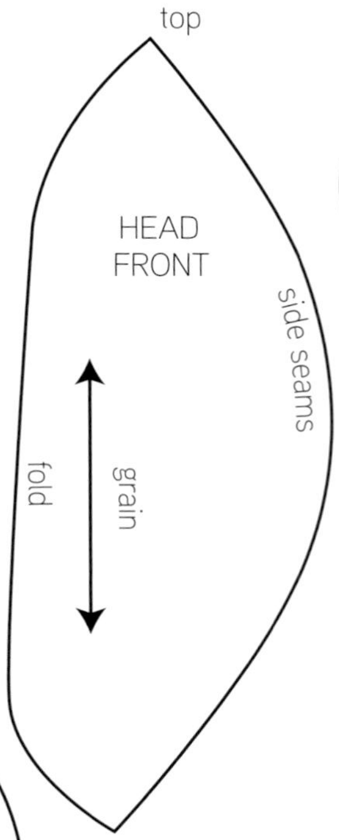

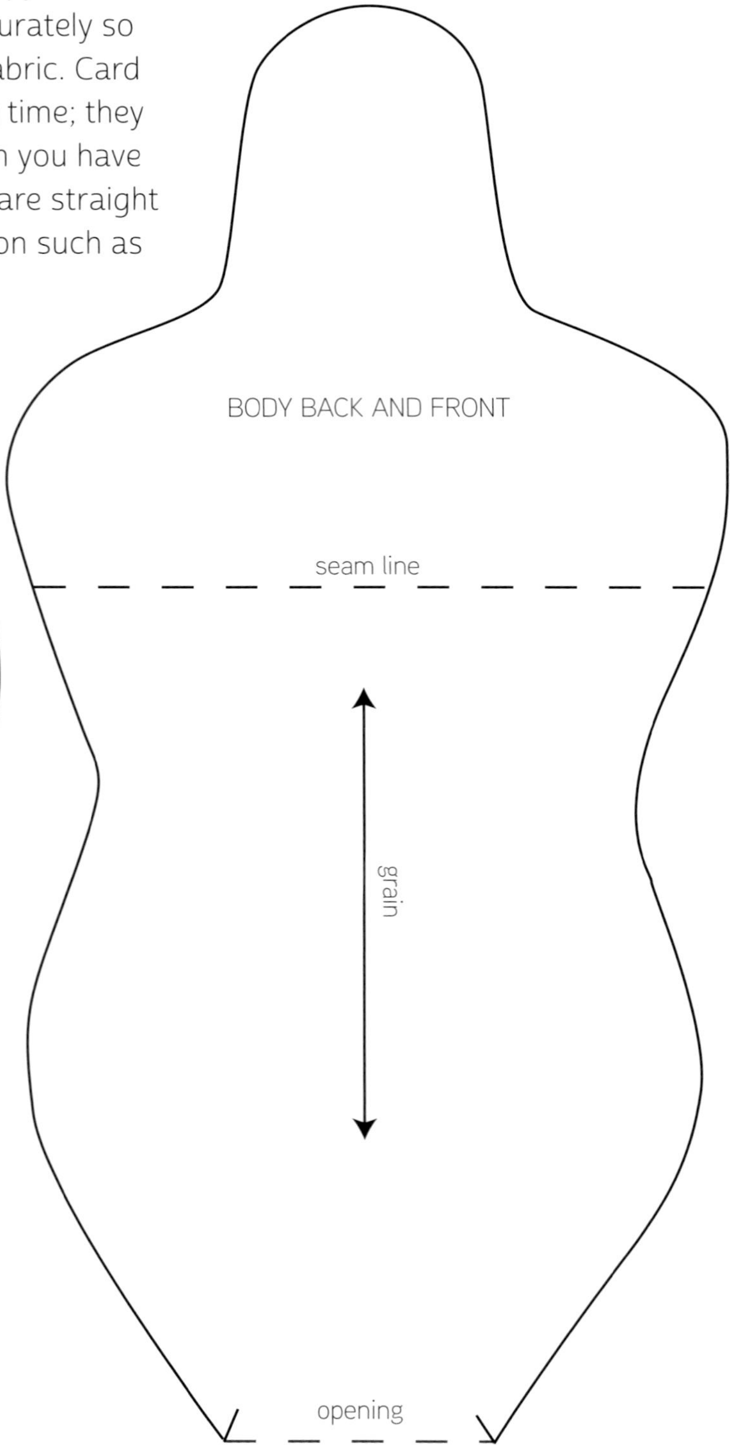

top

HEAD FRONT

side seams

fold

grain

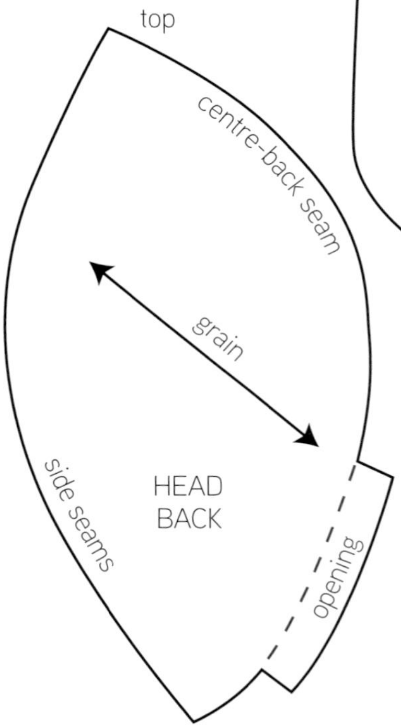

BODY BACK AND FRONT

seam line

grain

top

centre-back seam

grain

side seams

HEAD BACK

opening

opening

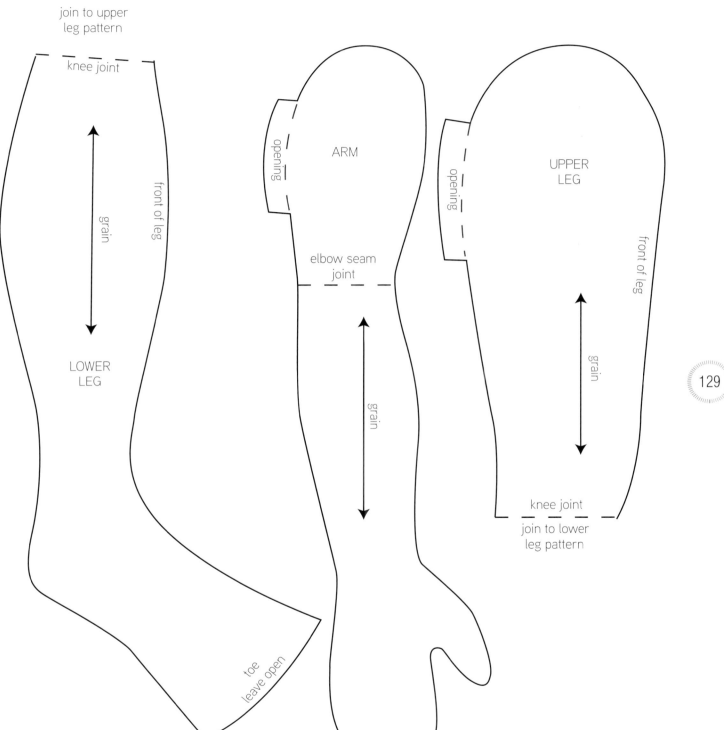

join to upper
leg pattern

knee joint

front of leg

grain

LOWER
LEG

toe
leave open

ARM

opening

elbow seam
joint

grain

opening

UPPER
LEG

front of leg

grain

knee joint

join to lower
leg pattern

Peaseblossom

and Moon Flower variation, pages 54–67.

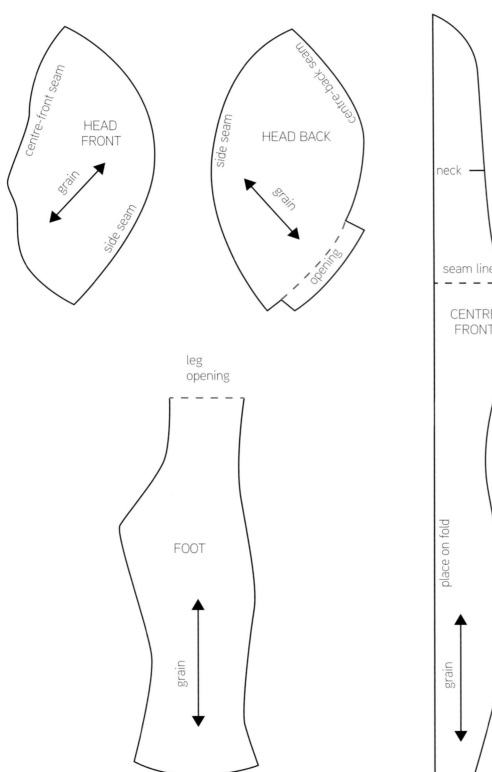

HEAD FRONT

centre-front seam

grain

side seam

HEAD BACK

side seam

centre-back seam

grain

opening

leg opening

FOOT

grain

toe
leave open

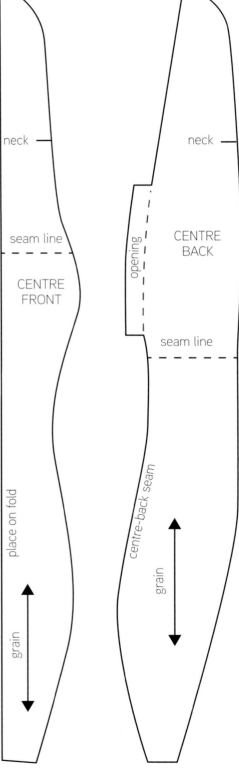

neck

seam line

CENTRE FRONT

place on fold

grain

neck

opening

CENTRE BACK

seam line

centre-back seam

grain

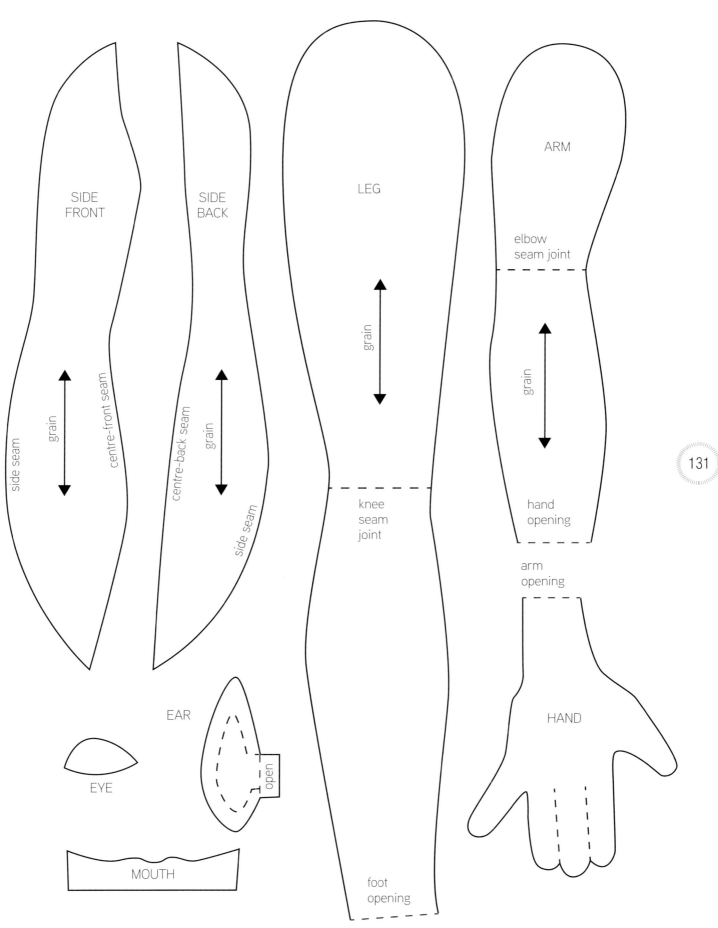

SIDE
FRONT

side seam

grain

centre-front seam

SIDE
BACK

centre-back seam

grain

side seam

LEG

grain

knee
seam
joint

foot
opening

ARM

elbow
seam joint

grain

hand
opening

arm
opening

HAND

EAR

open

EYE

MOUTH

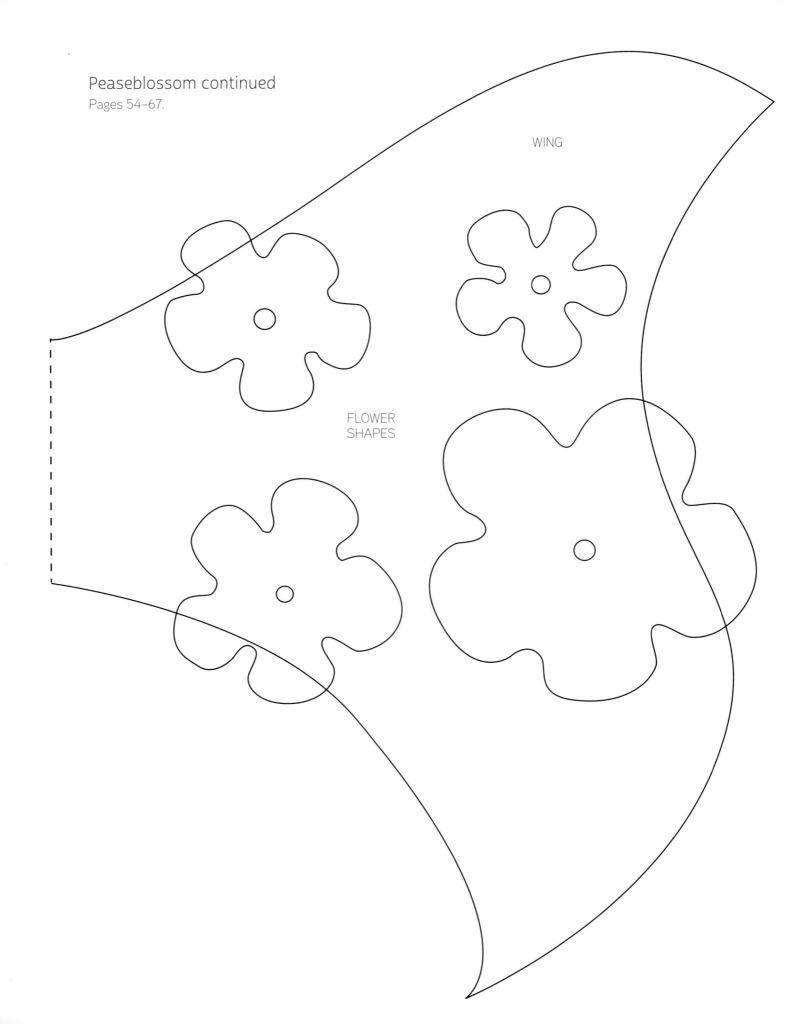

Peaseblossom continued
Pages 54–67.

WING

FLOWER
SHAPES

Anastasia

and Genevieve variation, pages 68–85.

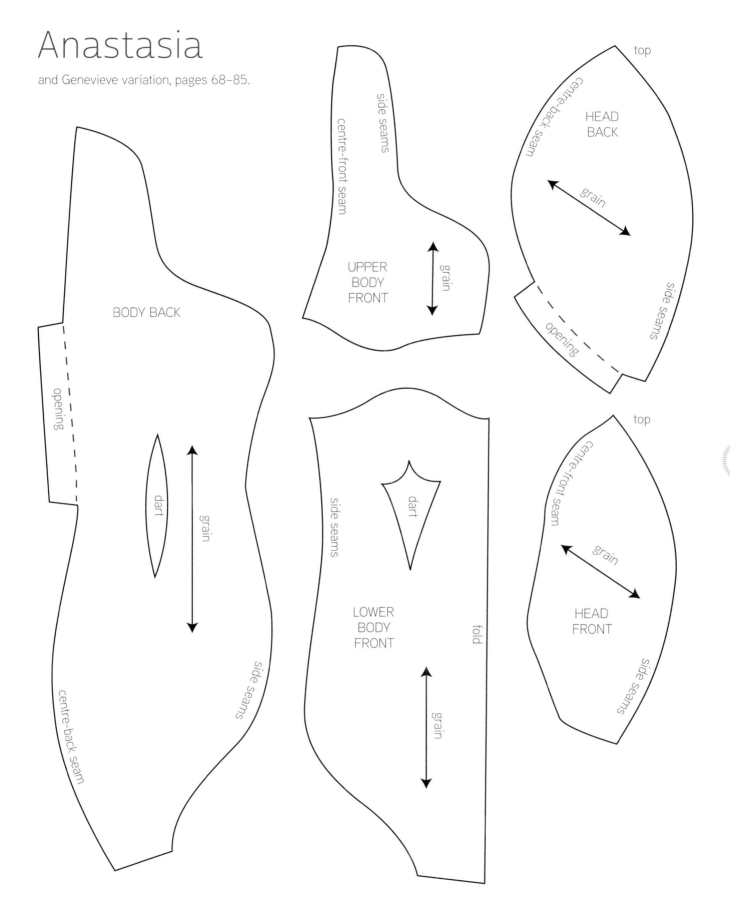

BODY BACK

opening

dart

grain

centre-back seam

side seams

side seams

centre-front seam

UPPER BODY FRONT

grain

side seams

LOWER BODY FRONT

dart

fold

grain

top

HEAD BACK

centre-back seam

grain

side seams

opening

top

centre-front seam

grain

HEAD FRONT

side seams

133

Anastasia continued
pages 68–85.

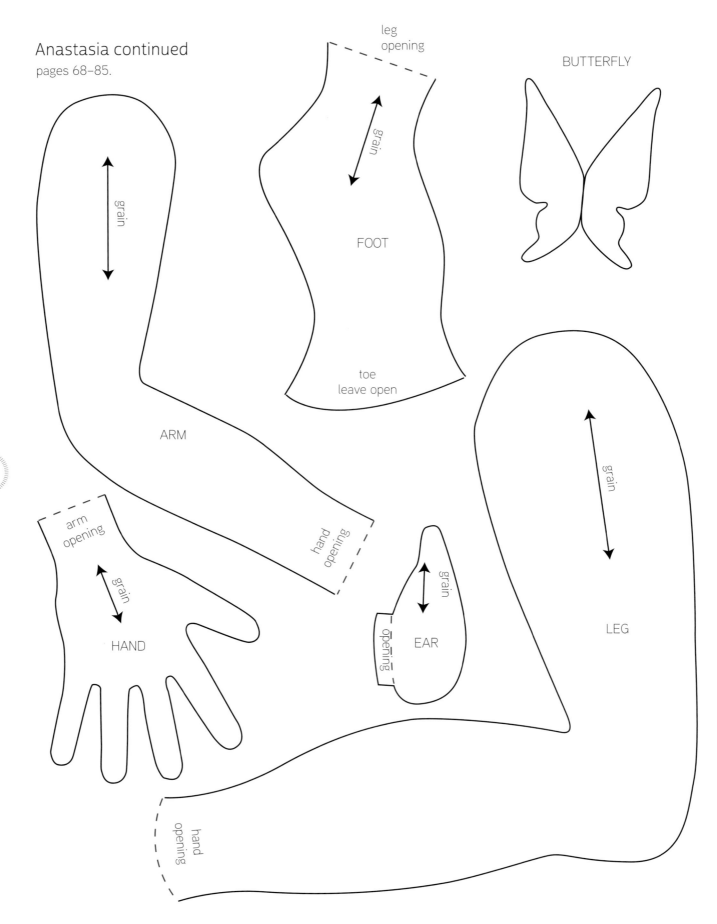

leg opening

BUTTERFLY

grain

FOOT

toe leave open

grain

ARM

arm opening

grain

HAND

hand opening

opening

grain

EAR

grain

LEG

hand opening

Morwenna

and Rhiannon variation, pages 86–99.

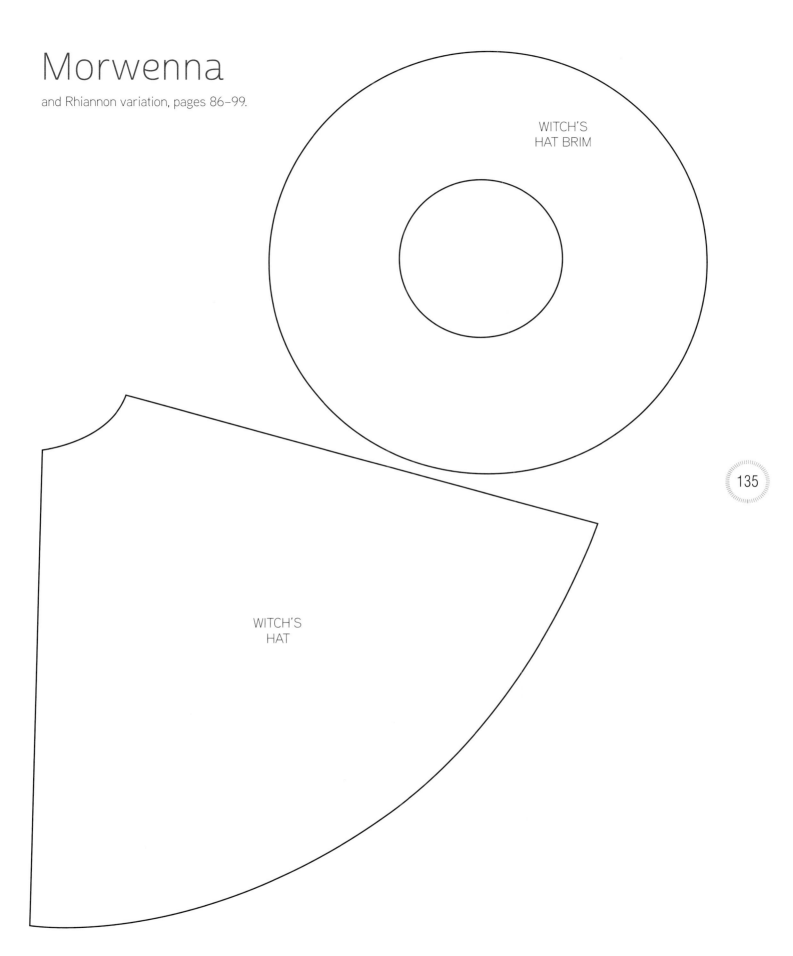

WITCH'S
HAT BRIM

WITCH'S
HAT

Morwenna continued
pages 86–99.

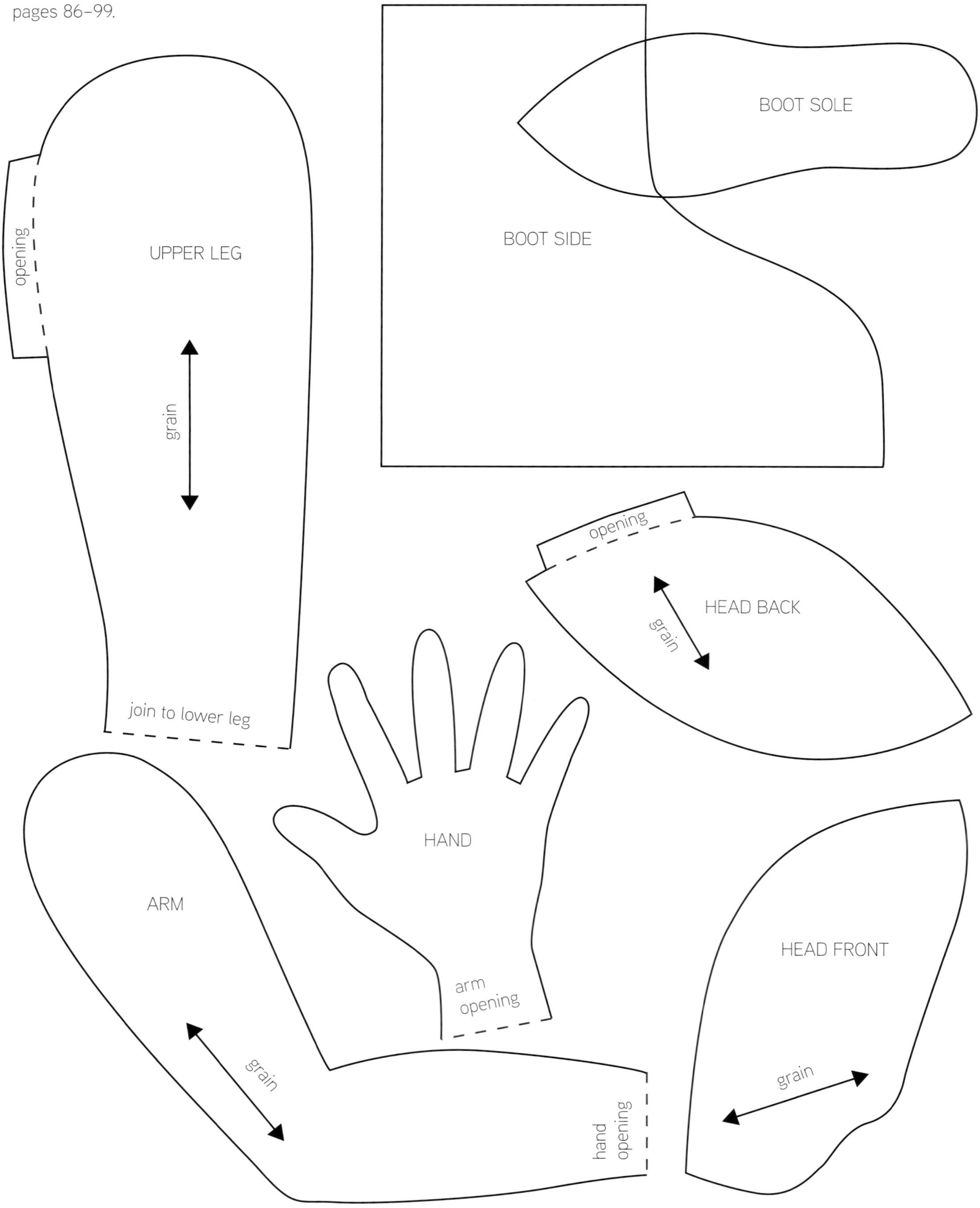

UPPER LEG

opening

grain

join to lower leg

BOOT SIDE

BOOT SOLE

opening

HEAD BACK

grain

HAND

ARM

grain

arm
opening

hand
opening

HEAD FRONT

grain

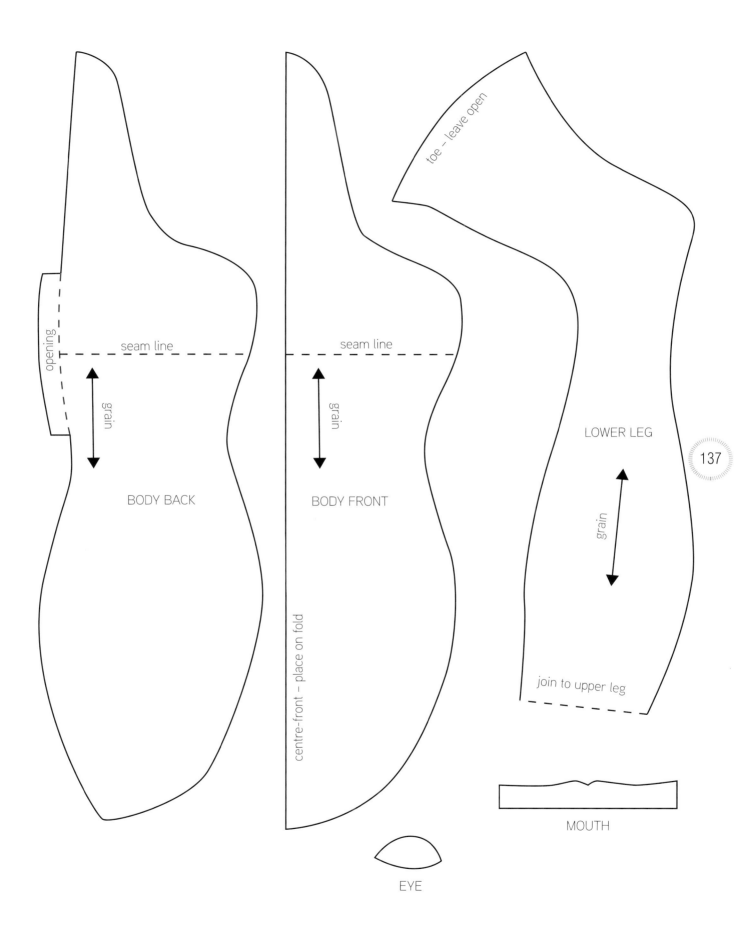

opening

seam line

grain

BODY BACK

seam line

grain

BODY FRONT

centre-front – place on fold

toe – leave open

LOWER LEG

grain

join to upper leg

MOUTH

EYE

Titania

and Coriander variation, pages 100–113.

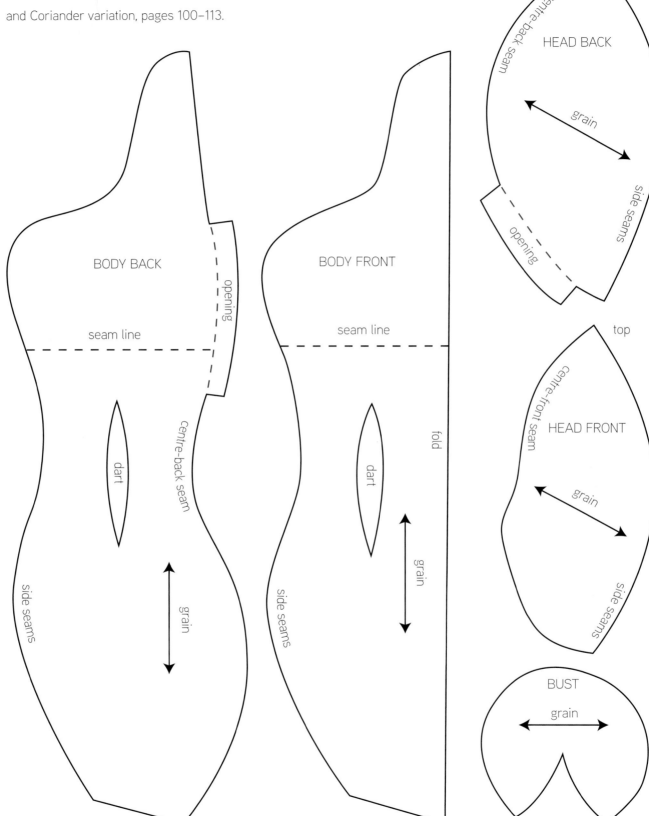

BODY BACK

opening

seam line

dart

centre-back seam

side seams

grain

BODY FRONT

seam line

dart

fold

side seams

grain

top

HEAD BACK

centre-back seam

grain

side seams

opening

top

HEAD FRONT

centre-front seam

grain

side seams

BUST

grain

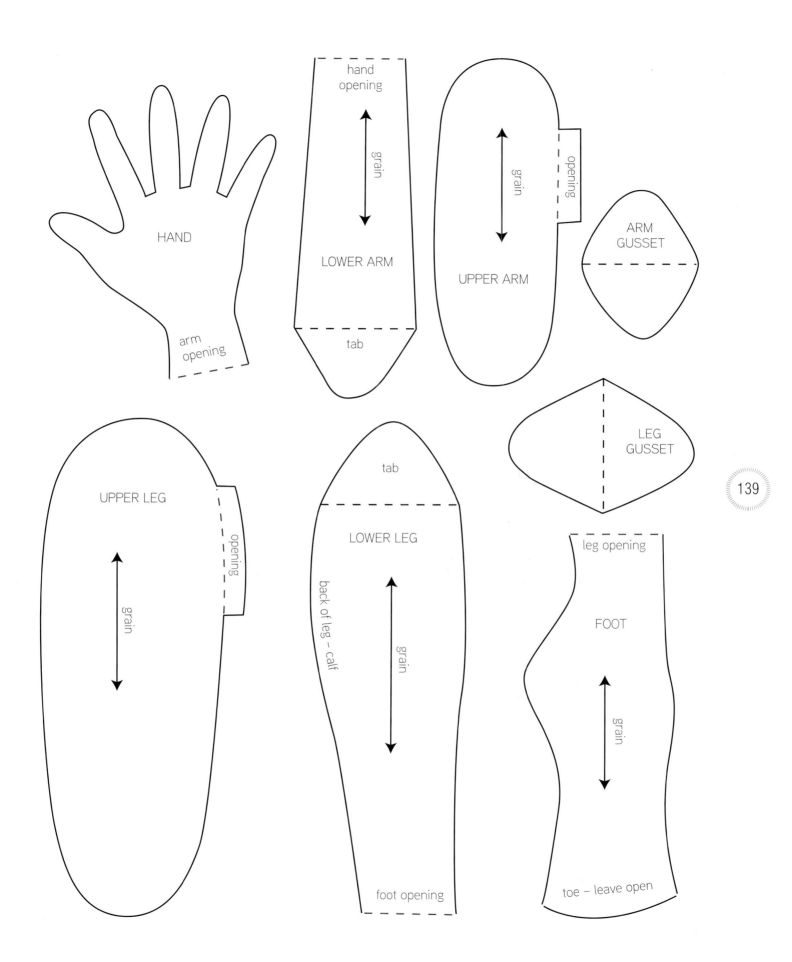

HAND

arm opening

hand opening

grain

LOWER ARM

tab

grain

UPPER ARM

opening

ARM GUSSET

LEG GUSSET

UPPER LEG

opening

grain

tab

LOWER LEG

back of leg – calf

grain

foot opening

leg opening

FOOT

grain

toe – leave open

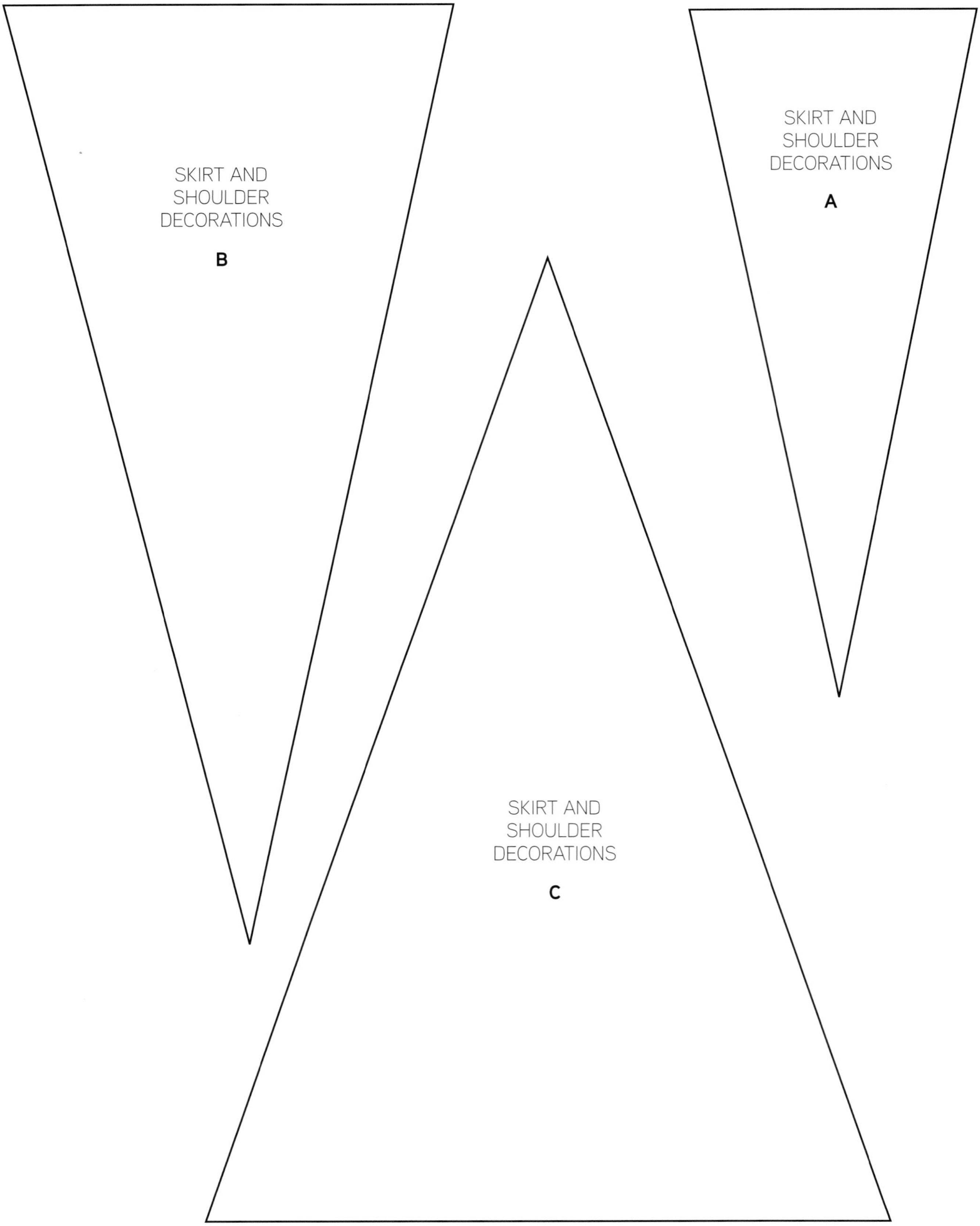

SKIRT AND
SHOULDER
DECORATIONS

B

SKIRT AND
SHOULDER
DECORATIONS

A

SKIRT AND
SHOULDER
DECORATIONS

C

TOP WING

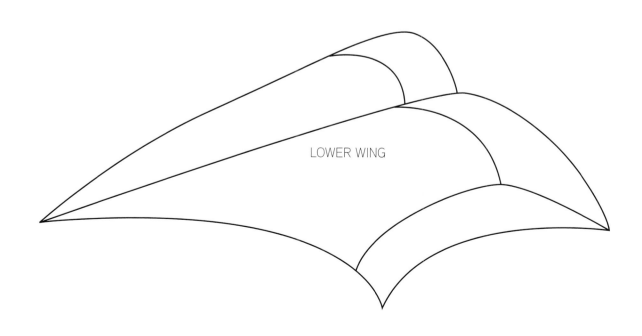

LOWER WING

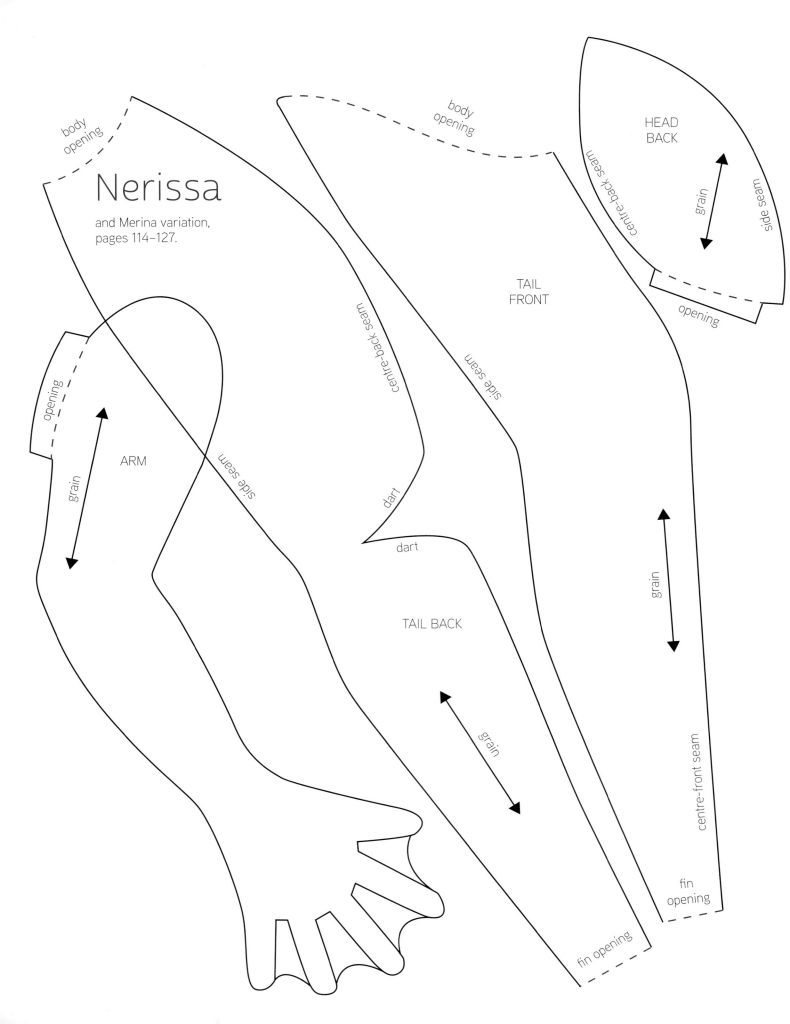

Nerissa

and Merina variation,
pages 114–127.

body opening

body opening

HEAD BACK

centre-back seam

grain

side seam

opening

opening

grain

ARM

side seam

TAIL FRONT

centre-back seam

side seam

dart

dart

grain

TAIL BACK

grain

centre-front seam

fin opening

fin opening

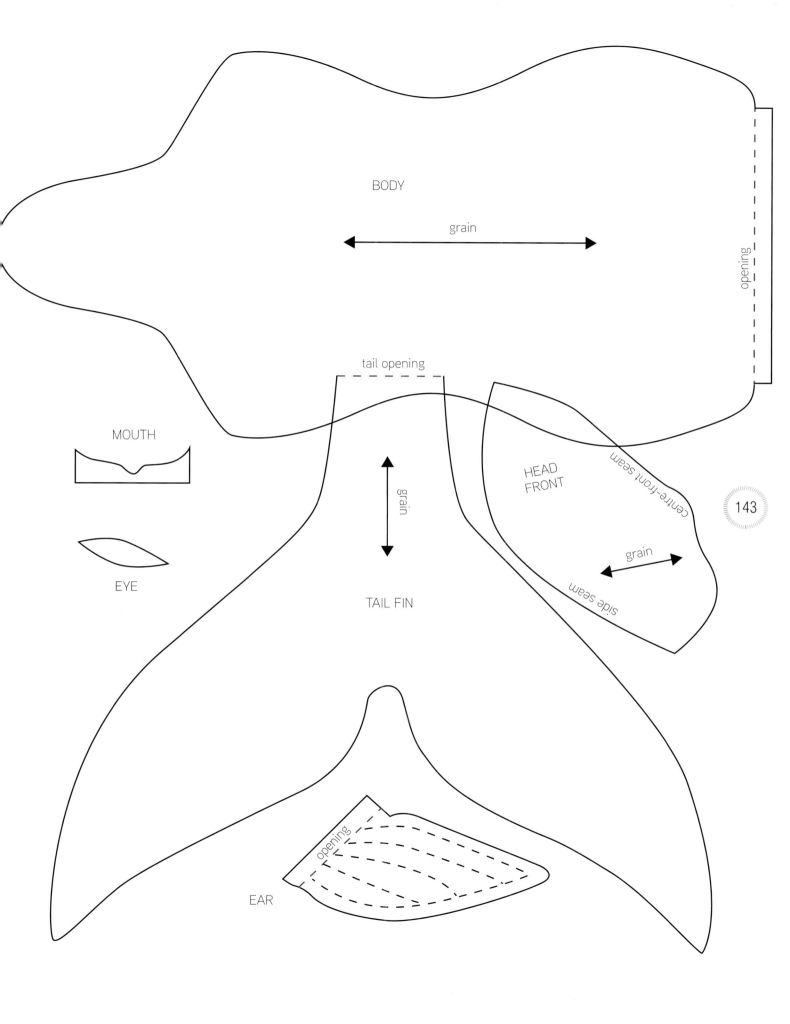

BODY

grain

opening

tail opening

MOUTH

EYE

HEAD
FRONT

centre-front seam

grain

side seam

grain

TAIL FIN

EAR

opening

Index

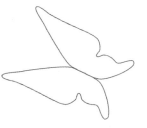